New Directions in Prose and Poetry 32

Edited by J. Laughlin

with Peter Glassgold and Frederick R. Martin

A New Directions Book

ACKNOWLEDGMENTS
Grateful acknowledgment is made to the editors and publishers of books and
magazines where some of the selections in this volume first appeared: for
Lawrence Ferlinghetti, *City of San Francisco* (Copyright©1974 by City Pub-
lications Co., Inc); for James B. Hall, *New Letters* (Copyright©1973 by James
B. Hall); for Steve Katz, *Epoch* (Copyright©1973 by Steve Katz); for Delmore
Schwartz, New Directions *Poets of the Year* series (Copyright 1941 by New
Directions Publishing Corporation).

The quotations from Alfred North Whitehead in Walter Abish's "In So Many
Words" are from *Adventures of Ideas* by Alfred North Whitehead (Copyright
1933 by The Macmillan Company; Copyright renewed 1961 by Evelyn
Whitehead). The translations of Franco Fortini's "Five Poems" appear in these
pages by permission of Arnoldo Mondadori Editore (Milan). The lyrics from
"Heartbreak, Tennessee" in Steve Katz's "Parcel of Wrists" are reprinted with
permission of Jack Music, Incorporated.

Manufactured in the United States of America
First published clothbound (ISBN: O-8112-0602-5) and as New Directions
Paperbook 412 (ISBN: 0-8112-0603-3) in 1976
Published simultaneously in Canada by McClelland & Stewart, Ltd.

New Directions Books are published for James Laughlin
by New Directions Publishing Corporation,
333 Sixth Avenue, New York 10014

CONTENTS

UPON READING
WILLIAM CARLOS WILLIAMS'S
PATERSON

MICHAEL McCLURE

SURE
YES,
PURE
POETRY
—like Blake rambling in the fields
or snakes by the lakes
where we raise high the shields
with our names.
Man, city, waterfall, panda,
are the same.
This April book is free
of shame!
And it dances
and glows
in the dark
of the Past

not far away.

THE EXECUTIVE TOUCH

JAMES B. HALL

ALLIED HIDE & SPECIALTY CO., INC.
1 TANNERY ROW
PENNINGTON, ILLINOIS

20 March 1972

(Mrs.) Barbara Blakey
2223 Country View Terrace
Pennington, Illinois

My Dear Barbara:

This letter conveys my heartfelt condolences to you, to Ed's immediate family in California, and to your boys who probably do not fully
understand all that has happened. Enclosed, also, are three checks
which pertain to your late husband's all too tragic severance from
ALLIED H + S.

First, Barbara, I want you to know all of us felt the funeral cere-
monies were exactly right: dignified, tasteful, well managed. The large,
non-Company "town" attendance confirmed Ed's value to our little community. I, myself, had not fully realized the extent of his personal
involvement: Indian Guides, Little League, and no less than three Pennington service clubs, including Rotary of which he was past-president.
These organizations will miss Ed Blakey's cheerful, affirmative presence.
To me, Ed's "outside" interests again underscored the vital role of our
company executives in bringing forth good community relations. In
Pennington, this was not always the case. Also, I hope you think one
big AH + S "All-Employees" blanket of carnations entirely appropriate
and not an hour passes that I do not ask the searching question, "How

2

shall AH + S ever replace our good soldier Ed Blakey?"

Why our Lockheed "Lodestar" crashed in West Virginia only a few miles from our newest tannery remains a mystery. The government team and our more flexible Flight-ops group under A. K. Carver are still investigating. No doubt the unexpected change in local, mountainous weather contributed. In any event, Barbara, AH + S maintenance work is always well in excess of minimum FAA standards. Those of us who also flew regularly in line of duty had the greatest confidence in both the Lockheed and her crew. Personally I doubt if the whole story will ever be known. Given the facts, I suppose we must accept the accident as one of life's necessary, tragic happenings.

The three checks enclosed are for you and your sons. The first check covers Ed's full month's salary (and allowances) even though the airplane crashed on 5th March. The second check of $15,000.00 will come as a pleasant surprise. Ed did not know it, but two years ago I contracted an "Accidental Death In Flight" program--at no cost to Company personnel. You and your family are beneficiaries of this company foresight. In addition, a third check of $4,000.00 is an administrative token of appreciation, a bonus for Ed's past services. My personal wish is that this amount be dedicated to the future education of your two sons. I hope you agree.

Meanwhile, I understand you will stay on in Pennington. I hope you will keep in touch. If problems arise, do not hesitate to call on me, just as though I were in fact a Godfather to Robbie and Mark. Oh yes, I nearly forgot to mention a minor item: two checks carry "Waiver Certificates" which are self-explanatory; our legal counsel routinely requires this sort of endorsement in all such cases.

Very sincerely yours,

J. KELLY JOHNS
President, and General Manager

Blind Carbon Copies to:
- Maurice Cohen, Finance
- Hack Bronson, Legal

ALLIED HIDE & SPECIALTY CO., INC.
1 TANNERY ROW
PENNINGTON, ILLINOIS

20 March 1972

(Mrs.) Gustave Lyons
R. F. D. Box 113
Millburgh, Illinois

Dear Mary:

It now being two weeks since the funeral I send my personal condolences. Enclosed find two (2) checks to cover your husband's terminal pay and allowances with AH + S for which he flew so many years.

I regret sincerely I could not attend Gus's funeral services at the United Methodist in Millburgh. Unfortunately, without consultation, Ed Blakey's services were scheduled here in Pennington at the same hour. I felt a prior obligation to accompany Mrs. Blakey and her two young boys to their father's funeral. I did, however, get out to Millburgh and personally left the Company's "All-Employees" spray of roses at the funeral home. Although less personal, I believe the closed-casket procedure was the best thing because all our men were pretty well bruised in the crash. In any event, I was with you at Millburgh in spirit.

The two checks enclosed are for you. The first check covers Gus's regular two-week pay period (and allowances) even though the airplane crashed on 5th March. The second check of $10,000.00 will come as a pleasant surprise. Gus did not know it, but two years ago I contracted an ADIF program--at no cost to company personnel. You are the beneficiary of this company foresight. I hope this little lift will provide additional financial security for you in the years ahead. Oh yes, I nearly forgot one minor item: the two checks carry "Waiver-Certificate" which are self-explanatory; our legal counsel routinely requires this sort of endorsement in all cases of termination.

As regards the probable causes of the crash, I can add nothing to what you have already read in the local newspaper. Company maintenance procedures are always well above minimum FAA requirements; unforeseen weather conditions all across Appalachia doubtless were a contributing factor. Probably we shall never know the precise truth.

In conclusion, I want you to know that all of us are going to miss Old Gus up there in the left seat of the Lodestar. He was a superb pilot; he knew the Lockheed well. Always cheerful, cooperative, and a fine man in every way, the Company will not soon find his replacement. Gus will be missed. I understand he was born and raised near Millburgh. I hope you think it fitting he should be laid to rest in the family plot.

Feel free to consult with me personally on any problems which may arise.

Sincerely yours,

J. KELLY JOHNS
President, and General Manager

bcc: Finance + Legal

ALLIED HIDE & SPECIALTY CO., INC.
1 TANNERY ROW
PENNINGTON, ILLINOIS

20 March 1972

(Mrs.) Ralph Shambrough
c/o Mr. Art Henderson, Apt. 12
5000 S.W. 59th Terracette
South Miama, Florida

Dear Mrs. Shambrough:

    This letter conveys my heartfelt personal condolences to you and
to Ralph's immediate family. Also I enclose two checks.

    First, however, let me state that I agreed wholeheartedly with your
decision to leave Pennington immediately after the funeral services. It
was very considerate of Mr. Henderson, Ralph's old friend from cadet
days, to bring his trailer to Illinois in order to move your house-
hold goods to his apartment in Miami. You are young. You will soon
make a new life for yourself in--I confess-- a more interesting area
than Pennington, Illinois.

    Although in his first civilian job, Ralph flew only a six-month
probationary period for AH + S, he was well-liked, always cheerful,
and showed great promise as a "Flying Executive." Although only twenty-
eight years old, Ralph had excellent military (jet) experience and
already had lived a full, exciting life. He brought a new military
alertness and tone to our whole aircraft operation. He will be
missed.

    The check enclosed is for you. The check covers Ralph's regular
pay as of March 5. Included also is a Company-paid ADIF insurance
check for $6,000.00, which will come as a pleasant surprise. You will
note a self-explanatory "Waiver-of-Claims" certificate on the reverse
of the check to be signed upon deposit.

    I hope these tokens of our appreciation for Ralph's past services
help you across the rough spots ahead.

                 Yours truly,

                 J. KELLY JOHNS
           President, and General Manager

MEMORANDUM

C O N F I D E N T I A L

TO: Sheldon Thomas, Vice President, Personnel

Dear Shell--

    This Memorandum (CONFIDENTIAL) in part confirms our prior discussion as regards replacements for: 1) Ed Blakey; 2) the two Lodestar pilots.

    1. RE NEW SALES MANAGER:

    Now I don't want to imply anything bad about the deceased, but let's learn something from the facts. Namely, our new Sales Manager must:

> a. Must <u>know</u> all product lines from our twelve tanneries, through our finish-plants and right on to final customer satisfaction. Blakey didn't. That's why I kept putting his ass on our airplanes, to get him out of Pennington and <u>to our production centers</u>.

> b. Must show 101 percent loyalty to AH + S management. Blakey didn't. More than once I asked him directly how much <u>company time</u> his Indian Guides, Little League and/or Rotary was costing me. I won't bore you with his justifications; I state unequivocally that Ed Blakey lacked a sense of proportion.

> c. Must be <u>cost</u> <u>and</u> <u>profit</u> <u>conscious</u>. Blakey wasn't. I grant his figures always <u>looked</u> good but the sales-costs for his so-called "Incentive Program for Excellence" contributed more to his personal popularity in the field than it put pure cowhide profits on our ledgers. In short, all of us carried both him <u>and</u> his "incentive" concepts. He was lucky to be so well known in Pennington--which is a very, <u>very</u> small town.

    Finally, I want to see final interviews with young, aggressive, straight <u>men</u> who won't whine and bitch just because it's a weekend and the weather is a little sour over West Virginia. On practically every flight this past three months I practically ordered Blakey to get on the Lodestar. A man that won't fly anyplace at any time won't well. Anything.

    Looking ahead: we will recruit a replacement <u>outside</u> AH + S: <u>do not promote from within</u>. That way we would only get another Blakey, small-bore.

    As a matter of courtesy I will ask Mr. Oaker for his New York recommendations. He owns other industrial interests and he gets around in both production and merchandising circles. I attach my own list of possible replacements. You may want to contact any or all of them in a preliminary way. I already gave you my new lower salary range for the job. Fringe as negotiated, of course.

    Now: let's get our new man aboard in thirty (30) days. A good Jew who knows leather might be the ticket, but no Californians. Not again!

2. RE NEW PILOT REPLACEMENTS:

Pretty much accept Carver's recommendations on replacements.
Again, we can learn something from the facts.

Gus was all right, but not much of an instrument pilot. He was
Senior pilot because in the old days he walked out of the cornfield to
fly a single-engine Fairchild for the previous company owners--well
before my time. We paid him plenty for sloppy flying, a "know-it-all,"
taciturn attitude which some customers found not easy to take. And
all of us were aware of his drinking habits. At the very least our
new Senior must be able to say "Sir" to a potential buyer without
making it a Supreme Court case re discrimination.

Looking ahead: we will promote from our present list, at an
appropriate salary savings (commensurate with Carver's judgment). In
addition, our new man should have the potential of Executive Leader-
ship and the ability to take over from A. K. Carver, if it comes to
that.

Re: Shambrough. No comment.

We might pick up a well-trained youngster who has been laid-off
by United or TWA. If he's local to Pennington, so much the better. No
more military types, please.

On balance, I see this terrible accident gives us a chance to
restudy our basic concepts (and costs) of AH + S versus Utilization of
Executive Aircraft.

Okay, let's crank it up.

                                        Cordially,

                                        J. K. J.

MEMORANDUM

C O N F I D E N T I A L and H A N D   D E L I V E R

<u>TO</u>: Maurice Cohen, Vice President, Finance

Dear Murray:

I dictate this at midnight, trying to clean up the mess of 5 March.
Here are some suggestions and facts (CONFIDENTIAL and HAND DELIVER) on
the financial aspects.

1. ACCIDENTAL DEATH IN-FLIGHT PROGRAM WITH EQUITY INDEMNITY (recap):

From prior conversations and Voucher Request Forms you know my decision
on reimbursing next-of-kin was as follows:

Blakey	$19,000.00
NB: in two checks, one ostensibly for an "Education" program	
Gus Lyons	10,000.00
NB: no minor children now alive	
Shambrough	6,000.00
TOTAL	$35,000.00

Since our specially negotiated contract with Equity Indemnity was
to insure any and all (undesignated) company personnel aboard (maximum
$250,000 per occurrence) at $40,000.00 per head, AH + S will collect
$120,000.00, and no questions asked. Thus we take down a favorable bal-
ance on this item of $85,000.00

Murray, I hope there is some way you can reflect that amount as
operating profit in the current year. I could use it for--as you know--
wholesale hide prices are killing us.

2. LOCKHEED "LODESTAR" N- 770 (recap):

I can be brief about that turkey: Legal confirms your suggestion of
the revised depreciation concept. That's a break. Good work. On insurance, Legal advises we are free and clear on any so-called reimburse-
ment at alleged "fair-market value." So we go for the whole amount,
and no questions asked.

Our coverage also has a provision for on-board <u>added</u> equipment.
Since Gus burned it all on the side of a mountain, let's confirm that
everything reasonable was "aboard." Two such items: first, A. K. Carver
had purchased some fancy new radio navigational gear, but--as is in-
creasingly usual with him--had not yet got the stuff installed in the
Lockheed. Let's say all of it <u>was</u> installed, even though you have to
predate a Work Order if questioned. Since we will never buy another
Lodestar, let's cash-out that specialized gear now. Secondly, let's
claim Blakey took with him on that last trip quite a few of his fancy
sales-promotion kits--which he may have, for all I know. AH + S has
plenty of cowhides tied up in that fancy little project and I strongly
suspect our replacement sales manager had damned well better have some
fresh approaches to a great many things around here. So let's peddle

a few of those kits to the insurance carrier. You handle it.

Looking ahead: I have had two opinions about our Operations (Aircraft): first, the Lockheed was about all Gus could handle. Therefore Carver allowed the sub-qualifications of one man to hinder a necessary company upgrading of our total flight Operation. Furthermore, we have been disappointed about the high maintenance costs on the Locky, not forgetting the fact that Carver actually wanted to replace both engines (Dallas Airmotive).

Secondly, our very tragic accident of the 5th of March now allows us to consider the question of a possible upgrading of the quality of all AH + S Executive Aircraft.

You have my Memorandum to A. K. Carver on this important issue.

I permit myself to say the following: A. K. Carver had better see this juncture in AH + S Operations (Aircraft) as an opportunity. At last, we need not bend our mature, managerial judgments to a situation we inherited from a previous, local, family-owned, two-horse tannery.

3. AIRCRAFT ACCIDENT and AH + S LIABILITY (Recap):

Legal worked up an appropriate "Waiver-of-Claim Certificate" for the reverse side of all next-of-kin checks. Legal doubts if such waivers are worth a damn in court but they may discourage plaintiff actions.

Legal is also of the opinion (I do not agree) that the Blakey woman might have a case, especially before a Pennington jury, on the grounds that I knew for a fact that the weather was sour, extraordinary late hour of departure, etc. Apparently the pilots have no case at all for either they contributed negligence or they failed to exercise due caution.

I expect no static.

You received carbon copies of my check-transmittal letters (20 March); I hope these well-calculated letters help smooth things over. Please make certain, personally, that those waivers come back to you duly signed.

Additional thought: contact your counterpart at the insurance office by telephone and confirm that they are under no circumstances to contact the next-of-kin. Their contract is with AH + S. The amounts we paid out are solely my executive decision. I think our settlements were fair and reasonable and in one case a little excessive for as you know Ed Blakey was on his way out. In other words, I want no post-payment awkwardness to cloud our future ADIF program. You handle it.

In conclusion, as we look down the road ahead, AH + S is now able to get stronger replacements for both Blakey and Gus Lyons, at a salary savings. Secondly, we cash-out an obsolete aircraft, and certain "inventories" aboard at the time while taking down a favorable cash balance of $85,000 on our little AIDF program. Finally, we can now re-think a new concept for all AH + S executive aircraft.

Well, it's late. I'm headed for the barn.

J. K. J.

MEMORANDUM

TO: A. K. Carver, Director of Operations (Aircraft)

Dear A. K.

I am turning down your recent policy suggestion to schedule AH + S aircraft for executive use only during daylight hours.

An airplane is no good on the ground. The cumulative expenses of grounding both personnel and aircraft at nightfall would be prohibitive. I am aware that some companies--not our competition--follow the scheduling policies which you ably suggest.

Al, I'm as sorry as you are about Gus's bad luck; I know you flew with him a long time in the Fairchild. Nevertheless, we have to rise above these things and carry on.

In this spirit please forward at your earliest convenience your recommendations for the acquisition of newer, possibly more appropriate equipment to replace the Lockheed. You may wish to recommend we step up to executive-jet aircraft. Faster, more efficient aircraft would give us a needed edge on our competition, but against this most of our plants, aside from Pennington and Mercer City, are in relatively isolated areas all across the Eastern Seaboard. Are company airstrips and/or nearby county facilities appropriate for business jets?

A. K., I will read your realistic list figures and recommendations with considerable interest.

In closing, let me express a firm conviction: all AH + S aircraft are extensions of the Executive/Sales thrust of your Corporation. All aircraft and flying personnel must hustle with the rest of us. Therefore short-notice flights at AH + S are routine. If we are not present first at the Sales-Opportunity Point, then all of us might as well remain grounded at the home office here in Pennington, Illinois. Time is of the essence in modern marketing. It is a fact: I ordered the Lodestar, crew, and passenger to report at once to our newly acquired plant in West Virginia. I had to do so on the evening of 5 March. I will do so again.

I expect your management of AH + S aircraft to implement the above goals each and everyday.

Very cordially yours,

J. KELLY JOHNS
President, and General Manager

Blind carbon Copies:
  - Maurice Cohen, Vice President, Finance
  - Seldon Thomas, Vice President, Personnel

ALLIED HIDE & SPECIALTY CO., INC.
1 TANNERY ROW
PENNINGTON, ILLINOIS

29 March 1972

Mr. Allen Oaker, Chairman-of-the-Board
Smyth-Oaker Investment Trust, Ltd.
505 Fifth Avenue
New York, New York

Dear Allen:

By now you have read the press accounts and have heard my pre-
liminary telephone report of the AH + S Lockheed "Lodestar" accident
not far from our newly acquired tannery at Healdsboro, West Virginia,
at about 20:00 hours, 5 March 1972. This is a letter of clarification.

Regards the proximate cause of the accident, I confirm the flight
was duly authorized (Pennington to Healdsboro, direct) and at this time
the investigation is not conclusive. Two facts must be stated: first,
the Lockheed carried an Instrument Landing System, including glide
path (and DEME); the strip at Healdsboro had only a radio beacon.
That tannery being a recent acquisition, our flight crew was not entirely familiar with the field. Secondly, in deteriorating weather
conditions, pilot error is indicated. They burned it approximately
five miles short of the runway.

I also lost Ed Blakey. Ed was a very gung-ho type. He flew off
on short notice to be in West Virginia for a morning new-product
(suede) conference. At the time I asked him if a telephone call and
forwarded suede samples would not suffice. Ed wanted personally to
see the new suede-run. So.

Regards follow-up action, I report the following:

a. The search for my new Manager of Sales (vice president) is
    underway. All of us out here wish to recruit outside
    AH + S: bring in new blood. If you have any personnel sug-
    gestions via your New York contacts, please advise.

b. My two pilots are being replaced.

c. Loss of the aircraft, added, equipment, and certain inventory
    items are adequately covered by insurance. After routine
    survivor disbursements, our ADIF program brings in approxi-
    mately $80,000.00

d. Regards long-range planning, I see this unfortunate accident
    as an opportunity to upgrade my sales management and also
    to upgrade pilot personnel. Finally, I am now in a position

to take a hard look at the overall efficiency of all our
aircraft operations.

On the final point, I solicit your usual astute advice. Your subsidiary is located in the middlewest: our present tanneries and finish-
plants are widely scattered. All-weather aircraft operation is a
necessity. What would you think of going to jet equipment?

Beyond the above merely local issues, you will be pleased to know
your company has moved steadily ahead in the specialty-leather field,
with sales currently 8 percent ahead of last year. The cost reduction
program you ordered when I took over out here is now paying dividends.
I anticipate an even greater share of the market in the next eighteen
months.

As to Company-Community relations, the turnout for Blakey's
funeral tells us his talent for community relations was both timely
and has served its purpose. Doubtless he created the new AH + S
"image" in this small town. At last the old-line, family ownership of
this business is now virtually forgotten.

The "new" AH + S being a fact, I look forward to more fruitful
company-community relationships, a genuine Partnership for Progress.

On a more personal note, I find small-town life a little
stultifying, as does my wife Lou. Still there are small-town rewards,
most notably the close, lasting ties which one inevitably builds. And,
as always, there is an interesting job to do.

Faithfully,

J. KELLY JOHNS
President, and General Manager

Smith-Oaker Investment Trust, Ltd.

505 Fifth Avenue
New York, New York

Dear Johns:

Off to Bermuda for ten days work/vacation with British interests. Nevertheless, want to answer your recent report of 29 March (about your aircraft accident).

You state my company lost on twin-engined airplane, two pilots, one Sales Manager, plus some "inventory" and still made money. I don't know how you did it, and I don't care. Don't try to bootlet the $80,000.00 into your <u>operating</u> profits.

By inference you have repeatedly complained about Mr. Ed Blakey, but because Pennington is a small town you lacked the guts to fire him. So you got a break: go out and find yourself a better man. I have no New York suggestions for a middlewestern based vice-president of Sales--in leather, or anything else.

Whether you upgrade your executive fleet of airplanes or not is entirely your decision. If a jet will make money, buy it; if it eats you up later, that's tough. Don't ask for a dime of financing from this end. I'd say exactly the same thing to any of my companies.

I remember Gus Lyons. A couple of times he flew me from Teeterboro out to Pennington. Very white hair, and chewed unlighted cigars. I thought he added a note of down-home cussedness to the whole proceedings. Sorry you lost him.

You state my subsidiary AH + S is making money. That's why I moved in on that down-at-the-haunch, family-run picnic in the first place. That's exactly why I hired you to run it. For your future health and welfare I suggest you continue same. Your expenses are still out of line in comparison to industry-wide practice.

If you don't like Pennington, Illinois, say so. I can always find someone else who either does, or will lie to me about it.

I've got to leave.

Thanks for the info.

J. A. Oaker

J. Oaker

At Home
2223 Country View Terrace
Pennington, Illinois
5 April 1972

Mr. J. Kelly Johns, President
ALLIED HIDE AND SPECIALTY COMPANY, INC.
1 Tannery Row
Pennington, Illinois

Dear Kelly,

Only a month ago this evening I got the terrible telephone
call from our local radio station, wanting to know did I have any
information about the airplane crash in West Virginia. It was Ed and
poor Gus, and Bob Shambrough. Now I am now pretty much "at home";
the neighbors have just been wonderful. The boys are fine.

I write to thank you for your thoughtfulness about the
three checks. You are generous to pay the full monthly salary; the
$15,000.00 really was totally unexpected. Edward never mentioned
such a program to me, so I doubt if he, himself, knew about it. The
"bonus" of $4,000.00 for the education of our two sons is a splendid
suggestion. I have signed the checks (and the waivers) and have
opened a bank account in the name of our sons. When they are older
you may rest assured I shall tell them the name of their benefactor.
Our heartfelt gratitude.

Looking back on it, I also feel the funeral services were
exactly as Edward might have wished. The cards and condolences from
all who knew him--including all of his Little Leaguers--are testimony
of the high esteem in which he was held not only by the community of
Pennington but also by his wonderful sales organization and their
wives.

Surely Edward was a kind, generous man. The future was
all before him.

I appreciate your willingness to be of further help. I will
come past your office a little later this spring to "talk things over,"
when my future plans are more settled.

Again, thank you for all you have done for us.

Sincerely yours,

Barbara Blakey

R. F. D. Box 113
Millburgh, Illinois
7 April 1972 (a Friday)

Dear Mr. Kelly Johns,

Rec'vd the two checks. They are cashed. Thanks a lot.

You weren't the only one that missed Gus's funeral. Since they
buried the Big Man in town at the same time, most of the Company
people went to his if at all. Except for the hangar bunch. They
came out here. Everybody. Maybe you like a closed-casked funeral,
but I do not. Now I'll always have to remember Gus the way he was
when he was called out on short notice that afternoon.

Which brings me to some points I want to make. I notice you
ordered Gus paid from the first to the 14th (normal two-weeks pay);
a big outfit like AH + S could have paid the whole month. But as
Gus said, "Why, naturally they skin everything." That's what
happened all right.

I signed your insurance check on the back not having much other
choice. But I know and Gus knew it wasn't absolutely necessary to
take off at five p.m. for a someplace in West Virginia he'd only
been to once before and that one time in broad daylight. But you
would have them go so they went. Gus called me at home from the
telephone in the hangar and said, "Don't hold your breath on this
one. Don't know when we'll get back." Well, that's what he was
paid for, I guess.

And I will say this. The newspapers always claim a "pilot error."
I will always think this one was caused by that high-time, right-
hand engine. If they was at altitude, in the overcast, and say the
blower went out, was there anyplace else to come down except on a
mountain? Maybe Gus wasn't the best on instrument flight but I
never did know him to be off any five miles on an approach. Gus
knew the whole U.S., and it's not like him to be lower than any
mountain, unless he knew for sure.

Well, what's past is past. If Gus had his choice he would always
have flown during daylight hours as he observed you pretty much
manage to do yourself.

Well thanks for the two checks and I've said in writing what's on
my mind. And my name is not Mary, it's Maxine, and always was.

                    Yours truly,

                    Maxine Lyons

                    (Mrs.) Maxine Lyons

ALLIED HIDE & SPECIALTY CO., INC.
1 TANNERY ROW
PENNINGTON, ILLINOIS

8 April 1972

(Mrs.) Gustave Lyons
R. F. D. Box 113
Millburgh, Illinois

Dear Maxine Lyons:

I received your letter of 7 April and advise since you have signed and cashed the settlement checks Mr. Lyon's salary account and his connection with the above-named company is terminated.

I have read carefully your thoughts on the possible causes of that tragic accident which saddened company personnel and the Pennington community. Nothing in the FAA or our own Company accident investigation reports substantiates your opinions.

Very truly yours,

J. Kelly Johns

J. KELLY JOHNS
President, and General Manager

FIVE POEMS

LAWRENCE FERLINGHETTI

STEPHEN

One night when it was very dark
    a certain Stephen appeared to me
                        in an epiphany
                            in the Caffé Sport
    (that same Stephen no doubt named
        after Stephen Daedalus
            by that generation of parents
                who named all its children
                    after the hero of
                        Portrait of the Artist as a Young Man)

and that same Stephen coming up to me
                        in the Caffé Sport San Francisco
            with a certain subversive air
                    of an arab with a scarab
    and showing me a color photo of himself
                            in the Caffé Trieste
                                three years ago
        looking like a young Pierre
            in the BBC version of *War & Peace*

and pointing out in a corner of the cafe
                    "the Greek chick I'm now involved with"
            whom he hadn't even met at the time of the picture
                ("the Greek *what?*" I asked him)
    but there they were
                    the two of them back then
        already "caught in the emulsion"
                        (as I pointed out to him)
        though the film not fully developed yet
                    the final print not yet made
    the print in fact still to be
                    put back in the developer
    to bring out the darker shadowed parts
                            of the total picture
        in which his fated resemblance
                    to a revolutionary Pierre
        or to a liberated Stephen Daedalus
                    would be made much much clearer
        and her fatal resemblance
                    to an Egyptian fertility goddess
                        made much dearer
    even as he strides forth to forge
                    "the uncreated conscience of his race"
        and even as he
                strode back to their table
        and I spied her through the Italian lattice
                        smiling so fatally at him
            and then kissing him
                        gratis

GREAT AMERICAN WATERFRONT POEM

San Francisco land's end and ocean's beginning The land the sea's
edge also The river within us the sea about us The place where the
story ended the place where the story began The first frontier the
the last frontier Beginning of end and end of beginning End of land
and land of beginning Embarcadero Freeway to nowhere turned into
part of Vaillancourt's "Wrecked Freeway Fountain" What is the water
saying to the sea on San Francisco waterfront where I spent most of

my divorce from civilization in and out waterfront hangouts China
Basin Mission Rock Resort Public Fishing Pier Harbor Lunch Tony's
Bayview Red's Java House Shanty Gallery Bottom-of-the-Mark Eagle
Café Longshoreman's Hall the Waterfront dead No Work No Pay Golden Gate Pilot Boat in fog Podesta Divers SS American Racer rusty
Mystic Mariner Motorship Goy Mount Vernon Victory Red Stack Tugs
standing out past the pier where I telephoned the lawyers saying I was
shipping out on the sailing ship Balclutha and wouldn't be back until
they tore down the Embarcadero Freeway along with the rest of
petroleum civilization and the literary-industrial complex far from
where I'm standing opposite Alcatraz by the thousand fishing boats
nested in green thick water The sea a green god feeding Filipino fisher-
men on the quays Hawaiians in baseball caps and peajackets retired
Chief Petty officers casting live bait Puerto Ricans with pile-worms in
tincans Old capital N Negroes with catfish called something else here
The top of Angel Island showing through fog funnelled through Golden Gate Monday morning October sun the Harbor Cruise boat tilting
with tourists into a fogbank Gulls on the roofs of piers asleep in sun
The Last Mohican eating his lunch out of a pail and catching his next
lunch with the last of it The phone booth where I telephoned It's All
Over Count Me Out The fog lifting the sun the sun burning through
The bright steamers standing out in the end of the first poem I ever
wrote in San Francisco twenty years ago just married on a rooftop in
North Beach overlooking this place I've come to in this life this waterfront of existance A great view and here comes more life The Western
Pacific Freight Ferry ploughing across the horizon between two piers
foghorn blowing as I ask a passing elderly ship captain in plaid suit
and Tyrolean hat for the time and he takes out his pocket chrono-
meter which says a quarter of two and tells me in thick Norwegian
accent "Qvarter To Tvelve" he just off a plane from Chicago no doubt
going to catch his ship for the Far East after visiting his aged mother
in Minnesota Foghorns still sounding at the Golden Gate An old
freighter light-in-the-water on headings adjusting its compass a pilot
flag up and the captain on a wing of the bridge coffeemug in hand
greatcoat collar up The wind beginning to come up blowing the fog
away from the phone booth the phone dial very clear All of Angel
Island now visible through the fogbank A red hull appears standing-in
loaded to the gunnels with oil An Arab on the bridge his turban flying
Passing Alcatraz he buys it The Last of the Mohicans reels in his line
On the end of it a string of beads once lost in a trade for Manhattan
Island The Belt Line Railroad engine stands snorting on a spur next

to the Eagle Café with a string of flats & boxcars I park on the tracks
imbedded in asphalt and enter the Eagle Café a sign on the wall saying "Save the Eagle—Last of an Endangered Species" and I get beer
just as old brakeman runs in and shouts "Blue Volkswagen bus!" I
rush out and save my bus from the train I see a clock and run for the
phone on the pier where the lawyer's supposed to call me back at
noon There's a dude in the booth with his address book out and a lot
of coins spread out on the ledge He's dialing ten numbers He's putting
the coins in very slowly He starts talking slowly He's really enjoying
himself The tide is running out The Balclutha strains at its moorings
The guy in the booth has a lot to say and lotsa time to say it He's in
his own civilized world enclosed in the booth of civilization and I'm
in mine outside waiting for my lawyer to call back with the final word
on my divorce from civilization Will they let Man be free or won't
they Will they or won't they let him be a barbarian or a wanderer if ·
he wants to I look at my reflection in the glass of the phone booth
outside It's like a mirror of the world with a wild me in it and the
Bank of America towering over behind me Will Eros or Civilization
win And who's this weirdo who is myself and where does he think
he's going to sail away to when there isn't any longer any Away
Another huge oiler stands in All the fucked-up diplomats of the world
on the bridge holding empty champagne glasses as in a Fellini movie
The guy in the booth hangs up and falls out I sit down in the booth
and drink my beer waiting for the phone to ring The Balclutha's
whistle blows The tide is at the ebb The phone rings

THE GREAT GROOVY CHINESE INVASION
OF NORTH BEACH SAN FRANCISCO

In the famous U.S. Restaurant
  in the last Golden Age of North Beach
listening to mafioso conversations
  interlarded with hardrock wingding jabber
  by Hongkong longhair streetgang studs
    with their choppers idling outside
while right-on Red Guards give the finger to
  Chinatown American Legionnaires and sweatshop mothers

with Taiwan real estate men in sharkskin suits
 advancing up the boulevards
  leading the Great Chinese Dragon on a string
And the ponderous Italian mamma telling me
      "Da bossa no lika da doggie"
 when my cockapollie barked under the table
       at an unbound female foot
And one thousand plastic chopsticks
 dropped straight down through the peeling ceiling
  staking everybody out in their undies
   right where they sat

DISSIDENTS

January bright sun
    tiny hummingbirds
      in the willows
  suddenly
   flittering up

as an ordinary American monster
     fourdoor sedan
 barrels up the canyon road
  backfiring & farting
    carbon monoxide

And the hummingbirds take flight
     in a flurry of fear
 a cloud of them all at once
     humming away
     into deep blue air
  where the sky sucks up
     their wing'ed hum
 and in the infinite distance
     eats them

Even as a crowd of huge defiant
>> upstart crows
> sets up a ravening raucous
>>> *caw ! caw ! caw !*

> and screams and circles overhead
>> and pickets the polluted air
>>> as the metal monster power-drives
>>> on up the canyon
>>> and over the horizon

And the crows now too
>> wing away on wind
> and are sucked up
>> and disappear
>>> into the omniverous universe

Even as any civilization
>> ingests its own most dissident elements

I AM YOU

Man half woman

> Woman half man

And the two intertwined

> in each of us

>> androgynous

> the limbs of one

> around the limbs of the other

>> clasping

my breast a vestigial remain

of yours

the heart a bivalve

clinging to a sea-cave

gyzm-foam blown
sea-foam blown
into womb's caves

distilled in flesh-vials
a million years ago
thrown up
out of the body of being
out of the sea's mouth singing

(silent seabirds winging over)

the sea incarnadine

As Saint Matthew's Passion
sung by a blind man
comes over the Sunday morning radio

And I am alone here
but if there were two of us
I would say

There is only one here
in the end as in beginning
one body breathing

And the body is us
the body is our selves
and I am you

SHENANDOAH

DELMORE SCHWARTZ

EDITORS' NOTE: The text of Shenandoah, *a verse play by the late Delmore Schwartz (1913-1966), has been long unavailable and is here being reprinted in its entirety for the first time since its publication twenty-five years ago. It was originally brought out in 1941 as part of the New Directions "Poets of the Year" subscription series (a shorter version had appeared earlier that year in the summer issue of* The Kenyon Review), *with the jacket "blurb" composed by the author himself.*

"The title of Mr. Schwartz's new work," he wrote, "suggests an American historical play. In a sense, but a deep and subtle sense, this is true. More than race and nationality are being melted down in the American pot: cultural and social values are also at stake—forces of many kinds, brought from the old world to be reshaped and revitalized in the new. Shenandoah *is the poetic record of such a process in operation.*

"The curtain rises on a name-day ceremony in a first-generation American family. A name must be chosen for a baby boy and a name is an important thing. How a name is more than a name—in how many ways—is the subject of the play; its action is the interplay of forces involved—rich material for a poet like Schwartz, whose special gift it is to make a blend of the real and the ideal which highlights the values in both."

To Francis Fergusson

It is the historic nature of all particulars to try to
prove that they are universal by nature—
—*Encyclopedia Brittanica*

Wer sass nicht bang vor seines Herzens vorhang?
Der schlug sich auf: die Szenerie war Abschied . . . .
—Rilke

(Enter Shenandoah, *to the right. A spotlight shines on him as the
theater is darkened and the curtain rises on a darkened stage.)*
SHENANDOAH. This was the greatest day of my whole life!
I was eight days of age:
Twenty-five years
Consume my being as I speak (for we
Are made of years and days, not flesh and blood),
And no event since then is as important!
In January 1914 a choice was made
Which in my life has played a part as endless
As the world-famous apple, eaten in Eden,
Which made original sin and the life of man
—Or as the trigger finger with a bitten nail
Which Prinzip's mind was soon to press
In Sarajevo, firing at Verdun,
St. Petersburg, Vienna, and Berlin—
And like the length of Cleopatra's nose,
And like the grain of sand in Cromwell's kidney,
As Pascal said, who knew a thing or two,
Or like the pinpoint prick which gave the great
Eloquent statesman lockjaw in the prime of life
(O Death is eminent, beyond belief!)
—Return with me, stand at my point of view,
Regard with my emotion the small event
Which gave my mind and gave my character,
Amid the hundred thousand possibilities
Heredity and community avail,
Bound and engender,
the very life I know!
(The stage lights up and the curtain rises.)

The curtain rises on a dining room
In the lower middle class in 1914:
Gaze briefly at the period quality,
Not at the quaintness, but at the pathos
Of any moment of time, seen in its pastness,
The ignorance which prophet, astrologist,
And palmist use as capital and need
—The dining room contains in vivid signs
Certain clear generals of time and place:
Look at the cut glass bowls on the buffet,
They are the works of art of these rising Jews,
—The shadow of Israel and the shadows of Europe
Darken their minds and hearts in the new world.
They prosper in America. They win the jewels
(My mind intends no pun, but falls on one:
Jews are no jewels, as Angles are no angels.)
Of cut glass bowls to place upon their tables,
Moved by the taste and trend of the middle class—

   (Enter Elsie Fish *with her child in a bassinet, and* Edna Goldmark,
her next door neighbor. Both are young married women, but Mrs.
Goldmark *is plainly the older of the two. As* Shenandoah *speaks,*
Elsie *is engaged in tending the baby, while* Mrs. Goldmark *regards
her.)*
Explain the other furniture yourself,
But lift your mind from the local color,
For the particular as particular
Is not itself, as a house is not its front,
And as a man is not his flesh:
                              Come now,
See the particular as universal,
Significance like sunlight, the symbol's glory,
As two crossed sticks of wood shine with the story
Of Jesus Christ and several institutions
—The union of particular and universal,
That's what one ought to see, as Aristotle
Has said for years:
                    he knew a thing or two—
   During the speeches of all the characters except Shenandoah,
*there is a systematic shift back and forth from formal speech to col-
loquial speech, a shift which is reflected in their actions, and echoed,
so to speak, in the shift from verse to prose.)*

ELSIE FISH. My father-in-law is coming to see me before the ceremony. I wonder what he wants. When he called, he was very disturbed and upset.

MRS. GOLDMARK. Maybe he wants to spend some time with his grandson before the ceremony. We do not know what it is to be a grandparent, we are too young. Just think, a grandparent has all the pleasure, none of the pain and expense.

ELSIE FISH. I do not think he is so pleased. This is no novelty to him. He has been made a grandparent five times already by his other sons and daughters. Do you know, he said it was a question of life and death that he wanted to speak to me about. What can it be? But he is always like that, always nervous, always disturbed.

MRS. GOLDMARK. Maybe he wants to speak to your husband too. Where is your husband now?

ELSIE FISH. How should I know where my husband is? Who am I to know such a thing?

SHENANDOAH *(standing at an angle to the scene, unseen and unheard).*
This marriage is a stupid endless mistake,
Unhappiness flares from it, day and night,
The child has been desired four long years,
For friends have told the young married woman
The child will change his father, alter her image
Both in his mind and heart. For he is cruel.
How can two egos live near by all their days,
If Love and Love's unnatural forgiveness
Do not give to the body's selfishness
and the will's cruelty lifelong *carte blanche?*

(A doorbell rings. The Negro servant girl passes from the kitchen at the left through doorway in back of dining room which leads to the hall.)

ELSIE FISH. That must be my father-in-law now. Since he has come about something very important, would you go now, Mrs. Goldmark, and come back when he has gone? You have been a wonderful neighbor.

MRS. GOLDMARK *(departing).* I have had two children myself. I know what it is to be a mother for the first time.

(Enter Jacob Fish, *a man of sixty.)*

JACOB FISH *(plainly preoccupied).* Dear Elsie, I was very anxious to see you before the ceremony. So this is my new grandson: what a fine boy! May he live to a hundred and ten!

SHENANDOAH. God save me from such wishes, though
     well meant:
This old man has not read Ecclesiastes
Or Sophocles. Yet he has lived for sixty years,
He should know better what long life avails,
The best seats at the funerals of friends.

JACOB FISH. My dear girl, last night I heard that you were going
to name the boy Jacob, after your dead father. Have you forgotten
that Jacob is my name also? Have you forgotten what it means to
have a child named after you, when you are still living?

ELSIE FISH. What is it, except an honor? An honor to you,
father-in-law, as well as to my dear dead father, although I admit I
had him in mind first of all.

JACOB FISH. Elsie, I do not blame you for not knowing the beliefs of your religion and your people. You are only a woman, and in
this great new America, anyone might forget everything but such
wonderful things like tall buildings, subways, automobiles, and ice-
boxes. But if the child is named Jacob, it will be my death warrant!
Thus all the learned ministers have said. It is written again and again
in various commentaries and interpretations of the Law. It has been
believed for thousands of years.

SHENANDOAH. How powerful the past! O king of kings,
King of the elements
               king of all thinking things!

ELSIE FISH. I am surprised that you accept such beliefs, father-
in-law. I never thought that you were especially religious.

JACOB FISH. Wisdom comes with the years, my dear girl. When
you are my age, you will feel as I do about these matters.

SHENANDOAH. This old man is afraid of death, though life
Has long been cruel as jealousy to him.
How often death presides when birth occurs:
Yet to disturb the naming of a child
Is wrong.
               though many would behave like this—
O to what difficult and painful feat
Shall I compare the birth of any child
And all related problems? To the descent
Of a small grand piano from a window
on the fifth-floor: O what a *tour de force*,
Clumsy as hippos or rich men *en route*

To Heaven through the famous needle's eye!
Such is our *début* in the turning world . . . .

ELSIE FISH. How can I change the child's name now? Some of
the presents already have his initials and his name has been announced
on very expensive engraved cards. What will I say to my mother, my
father's widow? This is her first grandchild. Do you really think a
name will make you die?

JACOB FISH. Elsie, look at the problem from this point of view:
why take a chance? If I die, think of how you will feel. There are
hundreds of names which are very handsome.

ELSIE FISH. Father-in-law, you know I would like to please you.

JACOB FISH. You are a good woman, Elsie. You are too good
for my son. He does not deserve such a fine wife.

ELSIE FISH. You do not know how he behaves to me. You would
not believe me, if I told you. I have not had a happy day in the four
years of my marriage.

JACOB FISH. I know, I know! He ran away from home as a boy
and has never listened to anyone. I tell him every time I see him that
he does not deserve such a wife, so intelligent, so good-looking, so
kind and refined!

ELSIE FISH. I will do what you ask me to do, I will change the
child's name. Jacob is not a fine name, anyhow. I want the boy to
have an unusual name because he is going to be an unusual boy.

*(The baby begins to howl, in a formalized way which does not get
in the way of the dialogue, but seems a comment on it.)*
You understand, I would not do this for anyone but you.

JACOB FISH. I will be grateful to you to my dying day!

ELSIE FISH. You have many years of life ahead of you!

JACOB FISH. You are a wonderful woman!

*(In this dialogue, the shift back and forth between formalized and
colloquial speech becomes especially pronounced.* Elsie Fish *hands
the child to* Shenandoah, *as if absentmindedly, and leaves the dining
room to go to the door with her father-in-law.)*

SHENANDOAH. She thinks to please her husband through
    his father.
Do not suppose this flattery too gross:
If it were smiled at any one of you
You would not mind! You might not recognize
The flattery as such. And if you did,
You would not mind! Such falseness is too pleasant:

Each ego hides a half-belief the best is true,
Good luck and sympathy are all it lacks
To make the bright lights shine upon its goodness,
Its kindness, shyness, talent, wit, and charm!
—In any case, what can she do? Fight Death,
The great opponent every undefeated
Except perhaps by Mozart?
                              As for belief,
To make a man give up but one belief
Is just like pulling teeth from a lion's mouth—
    (Shenandoah *turns his attention to the child in his arms, regards*
the child with lifted eyebrows and a doubtful smile. As he does so,
the spotlight falls on him, while the scene is left in a half-light.)
Poor child, the center of this sinful earth,
How many world-wide powers surround you now,
Making your tears appropriate to more
Than the un-understood need and disorder
Your body feels. True and appropriate
Your sobs and tears, because you hardly know
How many world-wide powers surround you now,
And what a vicious fate prepares itself
To make of you an alien and a freak!
—I too am right to sympathize with you,
If I do not, who will? for I am bound
By the sick pity and the faithful love
The ego bears itself, as if Narcissus
And Romeo were one: for I am you
By that identity which fights through time,
No matter what Kant and other skeptics say
—Is it not true that every first-born child
Is looked on by his relatives as if
They were the Magi, seeking Zion's promise?
At any rate, children for long have been
The prizes and the angels of the West,
But what this signifies let us omit
—Now in the great city, mid-winter holds,
The dirty rags of snow freeze at the curb,
Pneumonia sucks at breath, the turning globe
Brings to the bitter air and the grey sky
The long illness of time and history,
And in the wide world Woodrow Wilson does

What he can do. In the wide world, alas!
The World War grows in nations and in hearts,
Bringing ten million souls an early death!
—Forgive my speech: I have nor youth nor age,
But as it were an after-dinner speech,
Speaking of both, with endless platitutes—

(The spotlight goes out, the scene is once more fully lighted, Elsie
Fish *returns to the dining room with* Mrs. Goldmark, Shenandoah
*gives the child back to his mother, who acts as if he were not there,
and then* Shenandoah *returns to his position at the side, removed
from the scene and at an angle to both audience and scene.)*

ELSIE FISH. I felt for the old man and you know how I am: I always give in to my sympathies. I know it is a weakness. But what a
shame that he should let such beliefs make him afraid.

MRS. GOLDMARK. When one is old, one is like a child.

ELSIE FISH. And after all, I said to myself, he is a poor unhappy
old man who came to America because his children had come. His
wife abuses him because he does not work and his grown-up children
support him, but give the mother the money, so that he has to come
to his wife for a dollar.

MRS. GOLDMARK. That's the way it is, that's old age for you.

ELSIE FISH. But now I must find a new name for my boy before
the guests come. My husband's relatives are coming and some of the
men who work for my husband, with their wives. Mrs. Goldmark,
you gave your children such fine names, maybe you can think of a
name for me.

MRS. GOLDMARK. Thank you for the compliment. I like the
names Herbert and Mortimer more all the time. They are so distinguished and new and American. Do you know how I came to
think of them? I was reading the newspaper in bed after my first
boy was born. I was reading the society page, which is always so
interesting.

ELSIE FISH. Let's get the morning paper and we will see what
luck I have. I wish my husband were here, I must have his approval.
He gets angry so quickly.

(Mrs. Goldmark *goes into the living room at the right and returns
with the newspaper.)*

ELSIE FISH *(to herself)*. I wonder where Walter is.

MRS. GOLDMARK. Now let us see what names are mentioned
today.

SHENANDOAH. While they gaze at their glamorous ruling class,

I must stand here, regardant at an angle,
I must lie there, quite helpless in my cradle,
As passive as a man who takes a haircut—
And yet how many minds believe a man
Creates his life *ex nihilo,* and laugh
At the far influence of deities,
>   and stars—

MRS. GOLDMARK. "Mrs. and Mrs. Frederick Somerville sailed yesterday for Havana—" What a life! to be able to enjoy sunshine and warmth in the middle of winter: one would never have colds—

ELSIE FISH. Maybe some day you too will be able to go south in winter. Who would have believed we would all be as well as we are, ten years ago? Read some of the first names, one after another.

MRS. GOLDMARK. Russell, Julian, Christopher, Nicholas, Glenn, Llewellyn, Murray, Franklin, Alexander: do you like any of those?

ELSIE FISH. I like some of them, Mrs. Goldmark, but I might as well pick one from a whole many. Read some more.

MRS. GOLDMARK. Lincoln, Bertram, Francis, Willis, Kenneth—

ELSIE FISH. Kenneth: that's a fine name—

MRS. GOLDMARK. I don't like it: it sounds Scandinavian—

ELSIE FISH. What's wrong with that?

MRS. GOLDMARK. You should hear some of the things my husband tells me about the Scandinavians! Marvin, Irving, Martin, James, Elmer, Oswald, Rupert, Delmore—

ELSIE FISH. Delmore! What a pretty name, Mrs. Goldmark—

MRS. GOLDMARK. Vernon, Allen, Lawrence, Archibald, Arthur, Clarence, Edgar, Randolph—

SHENANDOAH. This shows how all things come to poetry,
As all things come to generation's crux:
Every particular must have a name,
Every uniqueness needs a special sound,
In the Beginning is the word,
>   and in the End
Gabriel will call the blessèd by their nicknames,
And summon up the damned by the sweet petnames
They called each other in adulterous beds—

MRS. GOLDMARK. Elliott, Thomas, Maxwell, Harold, Melvin, Mitchell, Tracy, Norman, Ralph, Washington, Christopher—

ELSIE FISH. I like those names, but none of them really stands out. How do you think they would sound with Fish? Washington Fish? Christopher Fish? I would like an unusual sound.

SHENANDOAH. She comes close to the problem's very heart,
She has a sense of connotation. But wrongly,
As if, somehow, she stood upon her head
And saw the room minutely,
                              upside down!
MRS. GOLDMARK. Do you know, I could read the society page
for weeks at a time? If I am ever sick, I will. I feel as if I had known
some of the members of the Four Hundred, the Vanderbilts and the
Astors, for years. And I know about the less important families also.
I know their friends and where they go in winter and summer. For in-
stance, the Talbot Brewsters, who are mentioned today: every year
they go to Florida in January. Mr. Brewster has an estate in the
Shenandoah Valley . . .
ELSIE FISH. Shenandoah! What a wonderful name: Shenandoah
Fish!
(The baby begins to howl.)
MRS. GOLDMARK. It is not really the name of a person, but the
name of a place. Yet I admit it is an interesting name.
ELSIE FISH. He will be the first one ever to be named Shenan-
doah! Shhhhh, baby, shhhhh: you have a beautiful name.
SHENANDOAH. Now it is done! quickly! I am undone:
This is the crucial crime, the accident
Which is more than an accident because
It happens only to certain characters,
As only Isaac Newton underwent
The accidental apple's happy fall—
(As before, the spotlight shines on Shenandoah, *the scene itself is
left in a half-light.* Elsie Fish *gives* Shenandoah *the crying child and
leaves the dining room with her neighbor.* Shenandoah *steps to the
footlights, goes through motions intended to soothe the crying child,
and speaks as if to the infant.)*
Cry, cry, poor psyche, eight days old:
Primitive peoples, sparkling with intuition,
Often refuse to give the child a name,
Or call him "Filth," "Worthless," "Nothingness,"
In order to outwit the evil powers.
Sometimes a child is named by the event
Which happened near his birth: how wise that is—
This poor child by that rule would thus be named
"The First World War"—
                              Among the civilized,

A child is often named his father's son,
Second and fresh identity: the wish is clear,
All men would live forever—
                    Some are named
After the places where they live, tacit
Admission of the part the *milieu* plays
And how it penetrates each living soul—
Some are called the professions, some are saints
As if to'express a hope of lives to come:
But everywhere on all sides everyone
Feels with intensity how many needs
Names manifest, resound, and satisfy—
The Jews were wise, when they called God
                              "The Nameless"
(He is the'anonymous Father of all hearts,
At least in *my* opinion). Legal codes
Are right too when they make most difficult
The change of names, flight from identity—
But let me now propose another use,
Custom, and rule: let each child choose his name
When he is old enough? Is this too great
An emphasis upon the private will?
Is not the problem very serious?

(The dining room fills with relatives and guests. Among those present are the infant's father, Walter Fish; Walter Fish's brothers, Joseph and Leonard, and their wives; Jacob and Dolly Fish, Walter's father and mother; Elsie Fish's mother, Sarah Harris, and her sister, Edna Harris; Jack Strauss and Harry Lasky, two men who work for Walter Fish, and their wives, Edith Strauss and Bertha Lasky. Shenandoah passes the infant in his arms to one of the relatives, and for a moment the infant is passed from person to person like a medicine ball, while everyone wears a broad grin. Then the infant is placed in his bassinet. Some are eating the sandwiches and fruits on the buffet, and Walter Fish gives one of the men a drink. An argument is in progress.)

JACK STRAUSS. To me, Shenandoah is a beautiful name, original and strange. I will give fifty dollars to be this boy's godfather.

ELSIE FISH *(to her sister, Edith)*. He is just trying to win favor with the man he works for.

BERTHA LASKY *(to her husband)*. What's the matter with you? Make an offer quickly: don't let him get ahead of you.

HARRY LASKY. I will give sixty dollars to be the boy's godfather—
JACK STRAUSS. I will go higher and make it seventy-five—
WALTER FISH. Gentlemen, Gentlemen: you will make me think
I ought to have a few children a week.

SHENANDOAH. Clearly these business men feel in the father
A man whose day will come: he will be rich,
They feel his power. They feel his strength. He is
A man whose friendship must be cultivated,
                              sought and won—
ELSIE FISH. Walter, you promised me. I want my brother Nathan
to be the child's godfather.

WALTER FISH. I promised you and I will keep my promise. Nathan is a fine young man, studious and intelligent. What better godfather could a child be given than a promising young doctor? *Nothing
is too good for my son.* Thank you, Jack and Harry, when the boy is
old enough I will tell him how much money you were willing to
spend to be the boy's godfather. No doubt, he will then feel kindly
to you.

SHENANDOAH. He has a brutal tongue, cannot resist
Speaking his brutal insights as if
No one else knew the human heart. Yet this
Proves that such motives are intense in him,
How would he know them, why would he mock them,
Smiling with keen pleasure when he sees them
At work in other hearts, except in great
Relief at finding colleagues, finding peers?

JACK STRAUSS. I bet the boy will make a million dollars—
HARRY LASKY. I bet that he will be a famous lawyer—
GRANDMOTHER HARRIS. I hope that he will be a famous doc-
tor—
SHENANDOAH. How utterly they miss the mark, how shocked,
How horrified if they but knew what I
Will one day be: if from their point of view
They saw me truly, saw my true colors,
                              grasped
And understood the rôle of my profession!
O, their emotions would approximate
Those of a man who has found out his wife
Has been unfaithful or was born Chinese—

*(Enter Nathan Harris, a good-looking and tall young man who has
recently become a doctor. It is obvious as he is greeted that he is well-*

liked and respected by all and as he shakes hands, his boundless self-assurance and sense of authority shows itself.)

NATHAN HARRIS. Where is my wonderful nephew, Jacob or Jacky Fish?

ELSIE FISH. Nathan, we have decided to give him another name since my father-in-law has the same name. We are going to call him Shenandoah—

NATHAN HARRIS. Shenandoah! How in a hundred years did you think of such a foolish name?

WALTER FISH. I fail to see anything foolish about Shenandoah?

NATHAN HARRIS. It is foolish in every way. It does not sound right with Fish. The association of ideas is appalling. The boy will be handicapped as if he had a clubfoot. When he grows up, he will dislike his name and blame you for giving it to him.

SHENANDOAH. How moved I am! how much he understands!
He is both right and wrong. He sees the danger,
But does not see the strange effect to come:
Yet what a friend he is to me, how close
I feel to him! He means well and he knows
How difficult life is,
                      climbing on hands and knees—

JACK STRAUSS. You are exaggerating, Dr. Harris.

HARRY LASKY. This is not a matter of the human body, in which you are an expert, Dr. Harris.

NATHAN HARRIS. No, not the human body, but the human soul: nothing is more important than a name. He will be mocked by other boys when he goes to school because his name is so peculiar—

SHENANDOAH. He is intelligent, that's obvious:
Perhaps his youth permits a better view
Of cultural conditions of the Age—

NATHAN HARRIS. Don't you see how pretentious the name is?

WALTER FISH. Nathan, there is nothing wrong with me. I am as good as the next one and maybe better. My son has a right to a pretentious name.

NATHAN HARRIS. Walter, to be pretentious means to show off foolishly.

(The infant has begun to cry again and cries louder as they quarrel.)

WALTER FISH. Thank you very much for explaining the English language to me. That's very pretentious of you—

NATHAN HARRIS. Excuse me, Walter: what I meant to say is that the two names of Shenandoah and Fish do not go well together—

WALTER FISH. I suppose you think something like Fresh Fish would be better? *(Laughter from the others.)*

NATHAN HARRIS. All right, go ahead and laugh. But if this helpless infant is going to be named Shenandoah, I don't want to be his godfather.

WALTER FISH. Don't do me any favors! Others are willing to pay for the privilege. I am glad that you don't want to be his godfather—

NATHAN HARRIS. I am glad that you are glad!

GRANDMOTHER HARRIS. Nathan, don't lose your temper. What a shame, to quarrel on a day like this: what will the minister think?

WALTER FISH. He has come here to insult me and to insult an eight day old child. Who do you think you are, anyway? Just because you are a doctor does not mean you are better than us in every respect—

ELSIE FISH. Nathan, you ought to be ashamed of yourself: you should have heard the fine things Walter was just saying about you and how he wanted you to be the boy's godfather. I was the one who chose the name of Shenandoah—

NATHAN HARRIS. Then you ought to be ashamed of *yourself!* I am not going to stay here another moment to see a helpless child punished for the rest of his life because his parents have an inadequate understanding of the English language—

(Nathan *goes out as everyone follows him, trying to stop his departure. The child is given to* Shenandoah *again. Spotlight and half-light once more, as* Shenandoah *comes to the footlights, trying to stop the child's tears.)*

SHENANDOAH. This is hardly the last time, little boy,
That conflict will engage the consciousness
Of those who might admire Nature, pray to God,
Make love, make friends, make works of art,
                         make peace—
O no! hardly the last time: in the end
All men may seem essential boxers, hate
May see the energy which drives the stars,
(L'amor che move il sole e l'altre stelle!)
And war as human as the beating heart:
So Hegel and Empedocles have taught.
—It is impossible to tell you now
How many world-wide causes work this room
To bring about the person of your name:
Europe! America! the fear of death!

Belief and half-belief in Zion's word!
The order of a community in which
The lower middle class looks up and gapes
And strives to imitate the sick élite
In thought, in emptimess, in luxury;
Also the foreigner whose foreign-ness
Names his son native, speaking broken English—
Enough! for this is obvious enough:
Let us consider where the great men are
Who will obsess this child when he can read:
Joyce is in Trieste in a Berlitz school,
Teaching himself the puns of *Finnegan's Wake*—
Eliot works in a bank and there he learns
The profit and the loss, the death of cities—
Pound howls at him, finds what expatriates
Can find,
        culture in chaos all through time,
Like a Picasso show! Rilke endures
Of silence and of solitude the unheard music
In empty castles which great knights have left—
Yeats too, like Rilke, on old lords' estates,
Seeks for the permanent amid the loss,
Daily and desperate, of love, of friends,
Of every thought with which his age began—
Kafka in Prague works in an office, learns
How bureaucratic Life, how far-off God,
A white-collar class' theology—
Perse is in Asia as a diplomat,
—He sees the violent energy with which
Civilization creates itself and moves—
Yet, with these images, he cannot see
The moral apathy after The Munich Pact,
The'unnatural silence on The Maginot Line,
—Yet he cannot foresee The Fall of France—
Mann, too, in Davos-Platz finds in the sick
The triumph of the artist and the intellect—
All over Europe these exiles find in art
What exile is: art becomes exile too,
A secret and a code studied in secret,
Declaring the agony of modern life:
This child will learn of life from these great men,

He will participate in their solitude,
And maybe in the end, on such a night
As this, return to the starting-point, his name,
Showing himself as such among his friends—

(The lighting changes as before, the whole cast comes back, and as the child is returned to the dining room by Shenandoah, *it is obvious that the argument has continued with greater and greater heat. For a moment, as the argument waxes fast and furious, the infant is passed from person to person hurriedly and painfully, like something too hot to handle.* Nathan *has been backed against the wall by his mother and several of the men, who are trying to keep him from making his departure.)*

NATHAN HARRIS. I say again that the name Shenandoah is inexcusable and intolerable, and I will not stay here unless the boy is given another name—

GRANDMOTHER HARRIS. What an unlucky thing for the baby, to have his godfather go away on this day: this day of all days—

WALTER FISH. Let him go, if he feels that way. He thinks he is too good for all of us—

ELSIE FISH. What name would you suggest for my child, Nathan? Just what is wrong with Shenandoah?

NATHAN HARRIS. I have explained again and again that Shenandoah is not a name, to begin with, and secondly, it does not go well with Fish.

MRS. GOLDMARK. He is just a snob—

JACOB FISH. I wish I had not started this whole business. But after all, a great tradition was at stake.

DOLLY FISH. You ought to be ashamed of yourself: you would like to live forever.

NATHAN HARRIS *(scanning the paper).* Mrs. Goldmark, you who are so resourceful, here, turn to the sport pages and read out the names of the entries at the race-tracks. *(Mrs. Goldmark turns aside in anger.)*

SHENANDOAH. My God in Heaven: what piercing irony,
To think of naming me after a horse—

NATHAN HARRIS. "Straw Flower, About Face, Cookie, Royal Minuet, Sandy Boot, Rex Flag, Hand & Glove, Fencing, Key Man, Little Tramp, Wise Man, Domkin—

SHENANDOAH. These names are fairly pleasant, after all:
But I am not the best judge, prejudiced—

WALTER FISH. This is too much: how long am I supposed to

stand here and be insulted without opening my mouth? To name my son after a horse: who do you think you are, anyway?

NATHAN HARRIS. Who do you think the child is, anyway?

(The child howls and Shenandoah *holds his hand to his head and then to his heart with feeling.)*

SHENANDOAH. I often wonder who I am, in fact—

WALTER FISH. Please depart from this house at once—

SEVERAL RELATIVES. Nathan! Walter! Nathan! Walter!

NATHAN HARRIS. This is my sister's home. I refuse to go.

WALTER FISH. I am going to get a policeman—

(Enter the rabbi, Dr. David Adamson.)

DR. ADAMSON. Ah, this is the house blessed by the birth of a child? what a wonderful thing it is to bring a human being into the world—

SHENANDOAH. Here is the man of God: what will he say?
How relevant are his imperatives?
Can he express himself in modern terms?
And bring this conflict to a peaceful end?
His insights, old as Pharaoh, sometimes work,
But there is always something wholly new,
Unique, unheard-of, unaccounted for,
Under the sun, despite Ecclesiastes—

DR. ADAMSON. But why did I hear such shouting and angry voices? What must God think, seeing anger in the house of a newborn child? Men were not born to fight with one another—

JACOB FISH. Why not let Dr. Adamson decide who is right?

WALTER FISH. This is my son: I am the one to decide his proper name—

DR. ADAMSON. A child is not a piece of property, Mr. Fish—

WALTER FISH. Are you here to insult me too?

DR. ADAMSON. Now, now: my remark was ill-considered: but let us get to the bottom of this improper quarrel—

ELSIE FISH. Let me explain quickly: we cannot name the child Jacob after my dear dead father because his other grandfather's name is Jacob, and here he is—

JACOB FISH. Thank God for that!

DR. ADAMSON. You are right, a child ought not to be named after a living man: that is the habit of the Gentiles.

JACOB FISH. Let us not imitate them—

ELSIE FISH. We decided to name him Shenandoah because that sounds like such a fine name. But my brother Nathan seems to think it is disgraceful. What do you think, Dr. Adamson?

NATHAN HARRIS. I wonder how much sense this anachronism has? He knows more than the father, however.

DR. ADAMSON. It is a most unusual name. There are so many fine names which belong to our people: why go far afield?

WALTER FISH. There has been enough discussion. I have made up my mind. The boy is going to be called Shenandoah.

SHENANDOAH. This shows the livid power of my father:
For fifteen years he will behave like this—

DR. ADAMSON. I do not want to add fuel to the flames of this regrettable dispute. I must admit that there is nothing seriously wrong with the name, although it is unusual—

NATHAN HARRIS. You see, he is not sure. He does not know. He would like to stop the quarrel, but he speaks without conviction—

SHENANDOAH. "The best lack all conviction, while the worst
Are full of passionate intensity—"

DR. ADAMSON. Young man, I am full of conviction.

WALTER FISH. Go on, Nathan, just go on like that: attack everyone in the house: did you ever see anyone so sure of himself?

ELSIE FISH. Walter, maybe Nathan is right, who knows? Why don't you call up Kelly and ask him?

SHENANDOAH. What a suggestion! fearful and unsure,
She seeks the Gentile World, the Gentile voice!
The ancient wisdom is far from enough,
Far from enough her husband's cleverness—

WALTER FISH. *All right;* everyone always says that I am unwilling to take advice and listen to reason. I will show you I can and I do. I will call my lawyer Kelly and we will find out what he has to say about the name. Not that I think for one moment that you're right, Nathan—

NATHAN HARRIS. Go ahead, Walter, call up Kelly: I won't think for one moment that you think I am right—

JACOB FISH. Who is this Kelly?

HARRY LASKY. Kelly is Walter's lawyer, one of the best young lawyers in town, one of the *coming* men. And they say he knows the right people in Tammany through his wife's sister—

DR. ADAMSON. Mr. Fish, to one and all it is perfectly clear that

that you have no need of me, since you have your lawyer Kelly. I would like to suggest that he perform the ceremony of circumcision—

(He starts for the door. Walter *stops him.)*

HARRY LASKY. Another one wants to go! Soon no one will be left!

WALTER FISH. Now, now, Dr. Adamson, no offense intended. With all due respect for you, you know it is always best to hear what everyone has to say. *After all, this child is going to live in a world of Kellys!* Just sit down for a moment while I call. I am going to make this worth your while.

DR. ADAMSON *(to himself).* Forbearance and humility are best: what good will it do for me to become angry? The modern world is what it is.

(Walter *goes out to call.* Dr. Adamson *helps himself to a piece of fruit from the buffet.)*

SHENANDOAH. His feelings have been hurt. The war between Divine and secular authority,
Is old as man in Nature! Ah, he knows
He is a kind of chauffeur and no more,
Hence he adjusts himself with a piece of fruit—

*(*Walter *can be seen in the hallway, holding up the telephone to his mouth.)*

WALTER FISH. Hello, Kelly: this is Fish. Fine and they're fine too. Nothing like being a father. And how are you? And the wife and children? That's good. Sorry to disturb you on a Sunday (hope you put in a good word for me with the Almighty! ha! ha!) I have a problem on my hands and I could use some of your advice (just put it on the bill, ha! ha!).

SHENANDOAH. For this did Alexander Graham Bell
Rack his poor wits? For this? Was it for this
The matchless English language was evolved
To signify the inexhaustible world?

WALTER FISH. You know today we are giving my boy a name. The ceremony is just like a christening, except that it's different— Yes, ha! ha!

NATHAN HARRIS *(to the rest, who are listening intently).* What a marvellous sense of humor—

WALTER FISH. I would like to have invited you, but you know how it is. Now the thing is this: we thought of naming the boy Shenandoah. Yes, Shenandoah: it seems to be some place down South.

But my brother-in-law is making a scene about the whole thing. He says the name is no good—

NATHAN HARRIS. As if it were merely a matter of opinion!

SHENANDOAH. Ah, what a friend! How close I feel to him! Almost as close as to that sobbing child—

WALTER FISH. I don't agree with him. It sounds fine to me, very impressive. But this is not the kind of thing you like to take a chance about. After all, a name is one of those permanent things. People will be calling him that every day in his life. O, now you're joking: sure, Francis is a fine name, but not for us. It would not go well with Fish—

NATHAN HARRIS. Inch by inch, against enormous odds, a certain amount of progress is, with luck, made now and then—

GRANDMOTHER HARRIS. Nathan, be quiet: no more fighting—

WALTER FISH. Now what do you think of Shenandoah, Kelly?

SHENANDOAH. Mark the dominion of the Gentile world:
This Irish Catholic will not quote Aquinas
Who wrote a treatise on the names of God—

WALTER FISH. Are you sure? All right, then Shenandoah it will be! Many thanks, and give my best to Mary: good-bye—

(Walter *returns to the dining room with a look of triumph.*)

WALTER FISH. He says it is a fine name, an elegant name. *He guarantees that it is a good name!* What have you to say now, Nathan? I suppose you think you know more than Kelly?

NATHAN HARRIS. I give up. No one can say I did not do my best—

WALTER FISH. Let's shake hands, Nathan, let's eliminate all hard feelings. I am sorry that I lost my temper. Some day the two of us will tell the boy about today and the three of us will have a good laugh about the whole thing from beginning to end—

NATHAN HARRIS. He may not share your sense of humor—

DR. ADAMSON. Yes! let kindness, forgiveness, good will, and rejoicing triumph in every heart on a day like this, the day which belongs to the first-born child.

NATHAN HARRIS. Here is my hand, Walter, but my left hand is for little Shenandoah!

(He *stretches out his left hand at an angle toward the bassinet.* Shenandoah *stretches out his hand to* Nathan. *But* Nathan's *back is turned.*)

SHENANDOAH. Nathan! here is my hand, across the years—

(Shenandoah *regards his unacknowledged hand with great sadness.*)
I am divorced from those I love, my peers!

DR. ADAMSON. This is the way that all conflicts should end.
They should end with a sacred rite. Nothing is so beautiful, nothing
is so good for the heart and the soul and the mind as a ceremony well-
performed. Let us go into the next room and begin the ritual of circumcision. The sacred nature of the rite will uplift our hearts—

JACOB FISH. This ceremony of circumcision gives me more
pleasure, the older I get, although I hardly know why. And after
that, the food and drink: no matter how old one is, that makes Life
worth living, if one has a good stomach—

SHENANDOAH. Prime Mover of this day, you are a card!
How many lives the Pleasure-Principle
Rules like an insane king,
                    even in dreams—
*(The men begin to go into the living room. The women remain be-
hind for they are barred from the ceremony. Shenandoah takes the
infant in haste and stands before the curtain.)*
They are about to give this child a name
And circumcise his foreskin. How profound
Are all these ancient rites: for with a wound
—What better sign exists—the child is made
A Jew forever! quickly taught the life
That he must lead, an heir to lasting pain:
Do I exaggerate, do I with hindsight see
The rise of Hitler?
                    O the whole of history
Testifies to the chosen people's agony,
—Chosen for wandering and alienation
In every kind of life, in every nation—

VOICE FROM THE LIVING ROOM. May the All-Merciful bless
the father and mother of the child; may they be worthy to rear him,
to initiate him in the precepts of the Law, and to train him in wisdom—

*(There is the sound of moving about and arranging and preparing
in the living room.)*
May the All-Merciful bless the godfather who has observed the cove-
nant of Circumcision, and rejoiced exceedingly to perform this deed
of piety—

(Again there is the sound of moving about and murmuring, then a pause and silence, while the faces of the women are turned toward the other room, full of pained sympathy.)

For thy salvation have I waited, O Lord. I have hoped, O Lord for thy salvation, and done thy commandments—

(There is an appalling screech, as of an infant in the greatest pain.)

And I passed by thee, and I saw thee weltering in thy blood, and I said unto thee, in thy blood, live. Yea, I said unto thee, in thy blood, live.

SHENANDOAH. Silent, O child, for if a knife can make you cry,
What will you do when you know that you must die?
When the mind howls with the body, *I am I?*
When the horrors of modern life are your sole place?
When your people are driven from the planet's face?
When the dying West perfroms unspeakable disgrace
Against the honor of man, before God's utter gaze?
Though now and then, like the early morning light's pure greys,
Transient release is known, in the darkened theater's plays . . . .

ORANGE SONNETS

GILBERT SORRENTINO

1   1939 WORLD'S FAIR

I still hear those azure carillons
floating from the Belgium building
caroming off the Trylon

and the Perisphere. Magic land.
Herr Dreyer grumbled because there was no
swastika. In "Florida" fake orange trees.

My mother was beautiful
in the blue gloom.
How she loved me.

Sore feet and headaches
Depression and loneliness
dulled her soft bloom.

She died ice-grey in Jersey City
with no solitary word.

2

Across this water sits a shore
patched together out of dim and smudgy colors.
It brings to mind a cartoon oddly porous.
Static on a worn-out sponge. Yet a core
of translucent light seems to spring
from the center of what looks a town or market
and drenches the lime-green haze of the park
I put there. One seesaw, one fountain, and one swing.

> Mothers and children in blue
> filled with good humor, china blue
> eyes and the rest, plus the sky is blue.

> You can see I'm trying to get there
> seriously. When I get there
> I'll be young again. I forgot orange. There.

3   IN MEMORIAM P.B.

Lavender, vanilla, anything.
The belt worn with such elegance
by the Mydas fly.

> How still. How still.
> Dusk ever. The rosy bridge.
> Everything is almost perfect
> In its name.

I give you the coronet, dead man.
Wear it in health. I never dream of you.
Vanilla. Orange ice. Un sombrero.
A lavish sunset soaks Brooklyn
With excruciating love.

> Kings.   Kings.   Kings.   Kings.

> Ah! The streets of dream

4

Now. Tell me how much I am to respect
the Prince of Orange. In that fine-spun prose
that fine-spun rosy prose.

How sheen it is! (Talk of dopey Raggedy Ann
hanging from a peg is talk
stained purple from sour grapes.

So they say. What a fine ring
(or is it twang?) the word "frivolous"
possesseth. Yea.

About dead Arthur. Who knows but I
that he loved licorice and
marshmallows?

Not you swell fellows and girls no no
Nor you swell girls and fellows

5   BROADWAY! BROADWAY!

Halloween is black and orange.
A song, as in "le clarinet du marmalade."
Some are happiest drowned
in a saxophone solo.

> "Le jazz hot" rhymes à la Mallarmé
> with tabasco: *vide* Bunk Johnson
> astomp in New Iberia.

> I saw Dexter Gordon play to six people
> in a frayed suit. His golden horn had lost
> its sheen. The notes gleamed.

Dexter in his brilliance.
Exquisite phrasing and perfect comedy.

A black velvet an
orange corona corona.

6
She was all in black. A statement
to take its place in "The History of Ideas."

We know black here in America.
Why, it's a scream.

Stick a point of orange in it
just for fun. Just to see what comes of it.

> After which: Prove that the light
> of bowling alleys is romantic.
> Is the very gravy of romance.
> "The *crème!*" yells a voice.

> Then, years later, drones the comic,
> I recall standing on a corner
> in the Bronx waiting for a bus.
> Yes, yes. Waiting for a bus.

7
She whom no one ever found
death found in Jersey City.

> Monsieur Mort, in a stupid play
> is a Frenchman of perfect grace.
> Politely he refuses orange ice
> with vanilla ice cream crowning it.

> He prefers *crème glacée,* eh? He
> smoketh Gauloises and Gitanes.

In the "film" they make of it
the plot is slightly warped.
Still, the gent simpers on and on
about his business. You know.

All in black with a French accent.
Plenty of crackling wit.

8   CANTA NARANJA
The sweet of dreams
is a Mexican Hat.
The sweet of dreams
a sombrero.
A sweet of dreams
on the street of dreams.
 Canta no lloro.

The sweet of dreams
is an orange hat.
The sweet of dreams
has vanillo.
One dreams of the sweet
on the street of dreams.
 Ay! Ay! Perdido.

TEN POEMS

ALEKSIS RANNIT

Translated by Henry Lyman

LONGISSIMUS DIES

This day was round
as fruits have
tender eyes.

Round as trees
were still,
      as words
              rustled.

MAGNOLIA GALLICA

I heard
the magnolias
long ago—

in the afterlight,
whitening
rain.

And now,
for once—
a summer's hour
in the dreaming dusk—
O great magnolia flower,
naked, blazoning
you.

RENOIR

Torsos,
like vases,
drink secretive music.

Some,
like your own,
flowering forth,

catch fire
in the white
from the crimson.

Renoir pours
into your sleep
this rounding light

shaded with rose,
till slumber is noon,
yours, the noon's heart.

But you, even
before he touched,
were vaulted sound.

DIMENSIONS OF VERSE

Melos within,
endlessly pouring
magical Eros without.

Master of music,
sober with joy.

WAITING

Last light of the westering rose,
beloved, rigorous tenderness,
harmonies held in repose,
profusion encompassed.

GRACE

The guise of shadow overgrows.
Lest radiance end in mold,
let rock be outward form,
the inward, springwater.

Springwater: the whispering idea,
the hearts's easy grace.

ALL SOULS' DAY

Und ich gehe die Allee allein,
leise . . .
—Rainer Maria Rilke

The Rilkean way,
pavements bitten soundlessly
by slow descending frost.

Poem—flame,
   downward
     cast.

Only a flame.

AT THE CARPENTER'S PLACE

  I have eaten at the altar stone
  and drunk the tempest
      from an angel's wings,
but never have I held a light more clearly limned
  than that engraved upon a severed branch
or born
  within a polished beam.

  And still these prayers
  fall silent in my hands.

THE MIRRORING HOUR

We seek the triumph of the dripping reed,
and hallowed by the sorcerous hour,

we purge the doubts that seared our days,
and hallowed be the rowing hour,

we silently call to the columns of clouds,
and hallowed be the mirroring hour,

we fall to our knees in a desert of waves,
and hallowed by the hour of grace.

OSCULUM

Clarity beginning
to dawn.

Now you
          and the willow
have a beautiful mouth.

IN SO MANY WORDS

WALTER ABISH

To J.

60

admires also America and apartment back bare be better between blue buildings can casual city elegant elongated exists extremely eyes far feet forth green immediately identifiable in instance is it large larger map mind note of on over parquet permit relationship replicating roving shape shining square stretched tall terrain that the this those to uncluttered underside unimpeded unspoiled wander windows

93

America is extremely fond of the casual relationship that exists between the underside of the bare feet and the shining parquet floor. It also admires the large windows (the larger the better) that permit the roving blue (note the blue) eyes to wander unimpeded back and forth over the uncluttered, unspoiled terrain, the terrain in this instance is also immediately identifiable on the map of the city, the elongated green square shape on the map replicating, if the mind can be stretched that far, the elongated windows on those tall elegant apartment buildings.

34

also America American are as brain but city come etc. every imprinted in institutions like live major mapped not of one only other outlines parks people streets the this to visit well who work

43

Like every other American city in America, the outlines of this one, as well as the major streets, institutions, parks, etc. are not only mapped but also imprinted on the brain of the people who live, work, or come to visit the city.

32

a an and at Bendel brain building coexists deep forth has her houses in into is like lives location looking map of office park peering she so that the where with which

47

In her brain the location of the park coexists with the building where she lives, and the building in which she has an office, and the building that houses Bendel, and so forth. Looking at a map of the city is like peering deep into the brain.

40

a absolutely and at America American building certain convulsed croissant eighth elongated floor four from height her delicious in intended irony is it Lee munching no of one perfection perspective quite Sara she splendor standing taking the true windows with

48

Standing at one of the elongated windows, munching a Sara Lee croissant (quite delicious) she is taking in the American perfection, the American splendor—absolutely no irony intended. It is true. From a certain height and perspective, the eighth floor of her building, America is convulsed with perfection.

48

a actually American and beasts below but city dogs dream eat few get go herd hoofbeats horses magnificent moment Nevada not occasionally of only open out people purebred snatch solitude spread taste terrain that the their them this those thundering to uninterrupted unspoiled vistas walk where wild yes

69

Spread out below is the unspoiled terrain where the city people go to snatch a few moments of uninterrupted solitude and dream of the thundering hoofbeats of the herd, the open vistas, the wild horses of Nevada. Yes, this is where the city people dream and walk their magnificent purebred dogs, those American beasts that not only dream of the wild horses, but occasionally actually get to taste them.

40

absorbing acutely akin all American and ant are aware constitute

crisscrossing dressing each foot framework gown her horse in indivi-
duals movement of on other outdoor people perfection tall terrain
that the they setting she sized something stands who window within
53

She stands in her dressing gown absorbing the movement of the
people who are crisscrossing the terrain, on foot, on horse, acutely
aware that they and all the other ant sized individuals constitute within the framework of each tall window something akin to perfection,
the perfection of an outdoor setting . . . the American perfection.
43

a Abercrombie able also and barefoot binoculars but by cheeks draw-
backs easily eighth enhanced exterior Fitch floor freshly from her if
interior is it male minor of on only parquet perfection rectified riders
see shaven she standing that the to unable use were
57

Is she also aware that by standing barefoot on her parquet floor the
exterior perfection is enhanced by the interior perfection. From the
eighth floor she is unable to see the freshly shaven cheeks of the
male riders, but it is only a minor drawback, easily rectified if she
were to use her Abercrombie and Fitch binoculars.
58

a against all America American are be cards cigarettes cheeks coffee
chrome deck dreamily expensive fence fond found freshly general
glass glossy heavy horseback in into is its large lazy leaning like mag-
azine men of on opulence or out pages perching reproduced rock
shaven smoking smooth some space spread staring table tall that the
thick those to who
76

America, in general, is fond of the smooth freshly shaven cheeks of
the tall men who are to be found on horseback or lazily leaning a-
gainst some large rock or perching on a fence, smoking a cigarette,
staring dreamily into the American space that is reproduced in all its
opulence on the pages of those thick glossy magazines that like a deck
of cards are spread out on the heavy expensive chrome and glass
coffee table.
26

also America American and are by fond Gillette good is made manu-
facturers more name names of popular products razor safety Schick
solid the they to two
34

America is also fond of the safety razor made by Gillette and Schick,

to name two of the more popular manufacturers. Gillette and Schick
are American products. They are also good solid American names.

19

a an Gillette her in introduction is legs morning once razor safety
shave she that the this uses week

22

This is an introduction to the Gillette safety razor that she uses to
shave her legs once a week in the morning.

41

a an and as available color colors compulsions daily dark dozen dread
drugstores everyone's handle in inexpensive is it lies many men model
most of on open popular prefer razor safety sell somber the their to
two unbreakable variety whole

58

The safety razor lies open to everyone's view. It is an inexpensive
model. It is unbreakable. It is a popular model and drugstores sell as
many as two dozen daily. The handle is available in a variety of colors.
On the whole, most men prefer dark colors, the somber colors, the
color of their dark compulsion and dread.

35

a acquired and as at attention bathtub bending blade down entire
firmly focused fresh gripped handle heightened her inserted ledge leg
legs on peering proceeded propping shave she significance slightly the
them time to yellow

44

She firmly gripped the yellow handle, inserted a fresh blade and proceeded to shave her legs. Propping one leg at a time on the bathtub
ledge, bending slightly, peering down, her legs acquired a heightened
significance as she focused her entire attention on them.

96

a acquaintance aglow ads American and another are assistance before
begin breakfast cannot cereal cheeks cigarette Crack Crackle Crunch
day encircled envy even evening faces for foreigners generally Gillette
goes good gripped habit have health hearty heavy her horse how image
in instead is it kick legs long men must next no of on one or packs
park place pose preference really ride Schick shave shaved she shortly
show slim solid smokers sometimes soon spitting stunning tall telling
that the their there they this those to took two usually visit want well
when who will with yes

130

This generally took place shortly before breakfast. Sometimes it took place in the evening. There is no telling when she will next shave her legs. Those stunning long slim legs that have gripped and encircled the spitting image of those tall men who pose for cigarette ads. Yes, her legs are well acquainted with those heavy cigarette smokers who cannot kick the two packs a day and ride a horse in the park before breakfast habit. America really goes for the hearty breakfast. Even foreigners on a visit soon begin to show their preference for one cereal instead of another. They want Crack Crackle instead of Crackle Crunch. How they must envy those good solid American faces. cheeks aglow with health, cheeks shaved with the assistance of Gillette or Schick.

61

a and anyhow as at away bathtub been but by cars clean comes daily for had have her hurry in intensity it ledge left love lying men must nine not of on office placed polish proper put razor repository safety same she show shiny somewhat that the their then they to up was weekend where white will wipe with woman

84

By nine she was at her office, the safety razor left lying where she had placed it on the white shiny ledge of the bathtub. The bathtub was not the proper repository for the safety razor, but she must have been in somewhat of a hurry. Anyhow, the woman who comes to clean up daily will put it away and then wipe the ledge with the same love and intensity that men show as they clean and polish their cars on the weekend.

37

and at bathtub bare discern dry fabricate feet gaze go her imprint ledge leg naked narrow occasional of on one only other rest shiny so speak standing that the to toilet using visitor will with yet

52

Will the occasional visitor using the toilet gaze at the bathtub ledge and discern the imprint of her bare feet, and then, with only that to go on, fabricate, so to speak, the rest of her standing naked on one leg, the other on the narrow ledge, the shiny yet dry ledge.

4

an incredible surface what

4

What an incredible surface.

2

incredible whiteness

2

Incredible whiteness.

4

of perfection the whiteness

4

The whiteness of perfection.

16

admonition bear by even is indefinite perfection repetition she tedium the troubled not of will Whitehead's

16

Is she troubled by Whitehead's admonition: "even perfection will not bear the tedium of indefinite repetition."

39

a adventure again although ardor brown but civilization costume essential first for intensity is it its learning light more morning namely new not of perfect perfection require search she sustains than the this to was white with wore Whitehead

46

This morning she wore a costume again. Although the costume was not white but a light brown, it was perfect. Whitehead again: "To sustain a civilization with the intensity of its first ardor requires more than learning. Adventure is essential, namely, the search for new perfections."

2

bathtubs new

2

New bathtubs.

31

ageless American apartment bring claim cleaning cleans enough every grain have her in ingredient is known lays object of old out polishes precious scrubs she surfaces that the to Whitehead woman

40

The cleaning woman is ageless. She polishes, scrubs, cleans to bring out the American grain, that precious ingredient that lays claim to the surface of every object in her apartment. The cleaning woman is old enough to have known Whitehead.

38

a an and artichokes bacon been Boston cereal chicken cigarettes cleaning coffee croissant Draino eggs envelope for frozen has in is Lee left lettuce list margarine money mushrooms next one peas Sara shopping soap spinach the to woman

43

The money for the cleaning woman has been left in an envelope. Next to the envelope is a shopping list. Eggs, coffee, bacon, cereal, mushrooms, Boston lettuce, Sara Lee croissant, artichokes, frozen peas, frozen spinach, one chicken, soap, margarine, cigarettes, and Draino.

41

a an anyone at aware bar boy did doorman driver elevator evening for freshly friend gloves had he her him his later legs man met neighborhood not of office old other plans shaven she tax the up was wearing white wondered

53

Was anyone aware of her freshly shaven legs, she wondered? Was the elevator man, the doorman wearing his white gloves, the taxi driver, the office boy, the man she met later at a neighborhood bar? He was an old friend. She did not invite him up. She had other plans for the evening.

24

admired although am an as costume did flat freshly friend hairdo her I invite legs me nasal not old shaven she up voice well

28

I am an old friend as well. She did not invite me up, although I admired her costume, her hairdo, her flat nasal voice, her freshly shaven legs.

43

a accustomed American an at briefly degree disappointed dry easily element every familiar firm go grip hand held how I in it let may meeting my not of perfection possess possession possessive quickly relinquished taking that thing to she some upon was would

62

Briefly, upon meeting, she held my hand in a firm grip. A dry possessive grip. A familiar grip. A grip that was accustomed to taking possession of every thing that may to some degree possess an element of perfection. It was a grip that would not easily let go. An American grip. I was disappointed at how quickly she relinquished my hand.

30

above all America America's and any are aroma cheeks fear had have her I into it legs limp many may men's not of perspiration prick running the unfounded unshaven were

41

Any fears I may have had of running into her were unfounded. America's fears are not unfounded. America fears the unshaven legs,

the unshaven men's cheeks, the aroma of perspiration, and the limp
prick. Above all it fears the limp prick.

41

a America America's American ardor be by can civilization clearly
fear first good he how in intensity is its keeps learning limp mind
more name of old paranoia prick referring requires states sustain sus-
tained than that the to when Whitehead wishing

53

America keeps Whitehead in mind. Whitehead is a good old American
name. When Whitehead states that a civilization wishing to sustain
the intensity of its first ardor requires more than learning, he is clearly
referring to America's paranoia, the fear of the limp prick. How can
ardor be sustained by a limp prick?

22

America America's and assistance do electric have how industries it
limp of prick produced razor revive safety that the toothbrush will
with

29

How will America revive the limp prick? It will do it with the assistance of America's industries, the industries that have produced the
safety razor and the electric toothbrush.

129

a action adventure alike also American and appearance are as aston-
ishing at belief beyond black bland blue braided brass bulging but
cap clean closer construction couple crotch Dad daily design differed
disfigured doing each eight elevator examination exceptionally faces
father floor foreign found from God good had hair haired have hand-
kerchiefs he heavy his I if in into is it jackets jeans leather like lips
looked looks man men must my noses nostrils not nothing number
obscene of off old operation on or ornate our other pants perfect
perfectly picture please proposals protruding puckered queers rose
said scribble slightly small specifically stain stains stared staring step-
ped still stood the three town troubled unanimously uniform urinate
walls was way were what white Whitehead who will with wondered
would yellow zippers

234

Whitehead would have found nothing astonishing or exceptionally
adventurous in the action of the three men who stepped into the elevator and said, eight please. The construction of the elevator and the
number eight were not foreign to Whitehead. But the three men were
foreign to the white haired elevator operator. He was troubled by

their appearance. Specifically by their black leather jackets. The jackets looked alike, but on closer examination differed in design from each other. All had heavy brass zippers. The elevator man was also troubled by their bland small town faces . . . by those puckered lips and slightly disfigured noses. What are they doing in my elevator, he wondered? If they had their way with this elevator they would scribble their obscene proposals on the walls, and then, to cap it off, they would urinate on the floor. A stream of yellow will stain the floor I clean daily. The crotch of their blue jeans is bulging beyond belief, thought the elevator man. They must have stuffed a couple of handkerchiefs into their pants. Those bloody queers. The three men stood staring at the old man. They stared at his braided cap, his ornate uniform, and at the stains on the ornate uniform, and at the white hair protruding from his nostrils . . . Good God, they thought unanimously. He looks like Dad. Our Dad. The picture of an American father. The perfect Dad.

49

American an and as bedroom bliss counting distance divides eight 8 extension 5 flat floor 4 grip had her horizontal in is joy line lips meantime of 1 pacing prairie pride 7 she steps 6 soon takes that the then thin 3 toward 2 turns was will window

71

In the meantime she was pacing the floor. The flat thin horizontal line that divides her thin lips is an extension of the distant horizon line in the prairie. She is counting, 1,2,3,4,5,6,7,8, as she takes eight steps toward the window, then turns and takes eight steps toward the bedroom. . . Soon her hands will grip the American joy, the American bliss, the American pride.

60

a after am American amiable an and are barstool bartender bring by class crack cracks democratization exchange first from Gillette greetings hands his I in introduction is it jacket knuckles left moist moment of on person pick Schick serve sitting sound spot suddenly surprise table takes the there third this tip to together we white wipe working up us yet

83

This is an introduction to the first person. I am sitting on the third barstool from the left. We exchange greetings. The amiable bartender in his white jacket suddenly cracks his knuckles. It takes us by surprise. Crack, crack, crack, the sound of American working class knuckles. The hands are there to serve us, to wipe up after us, to pick up the tip left on a moist spot on the table. Yet Gillette and Schick bring us together . . . a moment of democratization.

42

a all also and are bartender bartender's by cheeks design do each examine face fail for his I identical in is know knuckles longer morning my no not of one quarter razor safety she six smooth that the to use used uses

53

Each morning I use a safety razor that is identical in design to the one she uses, and for all I know, to the one used by the bartender. By quarter of six my cheeks are no longer smooth. I examine the bartender's face . . . I also do not fail to examine his knuckles.

20

a and body cake gently her I large legs mine of once same shave she soap soaped the watched using

30

Once I watched her shave her legs. Using a large cake of soap she gently soaped her legs. Using the same cake of soap she soaped her body and mine.

99

a actually also American an and apartment at barefoot Bendel blouse bought briefly buy by called car comes crash day dear deity doing dollar earrings ecstasy entire exotic familiar feeling feet fifty floor foot for four frequently friend from gallery grow has have height her hundred I in intended is it jade leaving mind moment natives of office on only overcome pair parquet perfect perfection personifies place plant pray presently print rainforest reaches Rosenquist seven she sheer spent spot spur standing stood Sumatra tall that the there three to told until uptown very visit was weekend what whom will

169

She spent the entire day at the office, leaving it only briefly to buy a Rosenquist print of a car crash at an uptown gallery, a blouse at Bendel, and a pair of jade earrings for a dear friend she intended to visit that weekend. She also, on the spur of the moment, bought an exotic plant. The plant is presently four feet tall. It comes form the rainforest of Sumatra. It will grow and grow until it reaches the height of seven foot three. In Sumatra the natives pray to the plant, she is told. The plant personifies a deity, and in Sumatra it is called perfection. She has the perfect place for it in the apartment. I have frequently stood on the very spot she has in mind. It is the perfect place for a three hundred and fifty dollar plant. Actually, what was I doing,

standing there? I was standing barefoot on her parquet floor overcome by the familiar American feeling, the feeling of sheer ecstasy.

53

a above achievement acknowledged all also America and applause ap-
probation ardor be bravery control dexterity each expects everything
for fucks general gifts give he herself his honesty in incredible in-
ventiveness is kind like loves man of passion people plant recognition
reward rewards self-control some stamina the their themselves time
to women would yes

73

The plant is a gift to herself. Daily people give themselves gifts in recognition of their honesty, bravery, and self-control. America loves
gifts. All gifts. America also loves rewards, recognition, applause, ardor, passion, and general approbation. Each time a man fucks a woman
he expects some kind of a reward for his incredible achievement,
his stamina, his ardor, inventiveness, dexterity and control . . . yes,
above everything he would like his self-control to be acknowledged.

34

a and away boats bundle cars everyone expensive fucked giving her
houses I liberally made one opera pajamas practiced ranches reward
rings self-control she shirts the tickets tidy ties time to used watches
who

37

At one time she used to reward liberally everyone who fucked her,
giving away expensive ties, shirts, pajamas, rings, watches, cars, houses,
ranches, and tickets to the opera. I practiced at self-control and made
a tidy bundle.

38

a advised although American an and at bought broken Common-
wealth competent complaining fucking gamely George have he I I'll
I'm it keep low me not of oil password preferred said shares the try
24,000 2¼ unusual up was

46

I'm not complaining. I have a competent broker. Keep it up, he advised me. It was the American password. Keep it up. I'll try, I said
gamely, although I preferred fucking George. I'll try, and bought
24,000 shares of Commonwealth Oil at an unusual low, 2¼.

44

and any around at bathroom come day did doing doorman down ele-
vator furniture her hoods in indescribable leave men messing might
moment neither night not operator or razors see slightly still that

the there them they things three to unspeakable were wielding worried up
63
The night doorman did not see the three men leave, neither did the day doorman, neither did the day or night elevator operator. It worried them slightly to see her leave, knowing that the three hoods were still up there, messing around, doing indescribable things to the furniture, doing unspeakable things in the bathroom. They might come down at any moment wielding razors.

85
a all an and another armpits at attention avoid bar behind breakfast bright but calls car costume costumes dark demanded desk did downward drink driver few for friend from glanced glasses good had hardly have her him home in invite into life looking making morning neighborhood never not of office old once other out place plans pretend ran rapid receiving regular sat seen shaved she shower some someone spotted spring stopped strokes tax the to told took tried unobserved up was went window with wore
135
She shaved her armpits with rapid downward regular strokes. She was unobserved. She took a shower, had breakfast, and went to her office. A bright spring morning. She sat behind her desk receiving a few calls, making a few calls. Some calls demanded all her attention. She wore another costume. She looked good in costumes, someone had once told her. She took a taxi home from the office. She had never seen the driver before in her life. She wore her dark glasses and hardly glanced out of the car window. She stopped for a drink at the neighborhood bar and ran into an old friend. She tried to avoid him, to pretend not to have seen him, but he spotted her. She did not invite him up to her place. She had other plans.

42
a an and anything as black designed elevator especially for her in incorporated into introduction is it jackets leather left men moment no of on one operator other plans rose said sank shaft stepped stood that the this three to use within
52
This is an introduction to the other plans. The plans incorporated the use of her elevator that rose and sank within a shaft especially designed for it. The operator stood on the left as the three men in black leather jackets stepped into the elevator. For a moment no one said anything.

10

admitted doorman elevator informed man men that the three were

12

The elevator man informed the doorman that the three men were admitted.

65

and apartment arrived at back be broken cleaning come company darned defaced disappointed door doorman elevator empty for from front furniture gone had have he hoods I'll Irma man may not nothing of opened operator out place report room said seemed she sounding ten that the their then to until unwelcome upstairs waited waiting walls wangs was wasn't watch well were when with woman you

84

Watch out, Irma, said the doorman to the cleaning woman when she arrived at ten. You may have unwelcome company waiting for you upstairs with their wangs out. The elevator man waited until Irma had opened the front door and then waited and waited until she had gone from room to room and come back to report that the apartment was empty. The walls were not defaced, the furniture wasn't broken, nothing seemed out of place. Well, I'll be darned, he said, sounding disappointed.

123

a after alike all almost although always an and another answer answering anxiety as ask at barely be behind brought but buttons cab call callousness carefully closet coffee communication costumes could depend desk did disagreeable dozen downpour due ear eight even eyebrows exuded faint find frequently had hanging her hour if in indifference inquiry insecurity instantly invite it juice left lift line lips long mahogany make many marmalade morning need not occasionally occur of office on one or orange parted plucked pressed put receiver respects sat say secretary secretary's selected selection share she shower similar simply slice so sound take telephone that the their thin three time to toast together toneless two very voice was went were when white with world would yes

216

She carefully plucked her eyebrows in the morning. Plucked them as if she had all the time in the world. She had a slice of toast with marmalade, orange juice, and coffee after her shower. She selected one of the two or three dozen costumes hanging in her closet. The selection did not take very long. In many respects, all the costumes were so similar, so alike. She went to the office. She sat behind her mahogany desk. Occasionally she would lift the receiver of her telephone and answer a call or make one. When answering a call, she would simply say, yes. The yes, a flat and almost toneless sound, was an inquiry, a line of communication that barely parted her thin lips. The white telephone had eight buttons. One of the buttons, when pressed, instantly brought to her ear the faint anxiety in her secretary's voice. She did not find the anxiety and insecurity her secretary exuded at all disagreeable. She could depend on her secretary. She could always ask her to put in another hour if need be. Although she frequently left together with her secretary, it would not, even in a downpour, occur to her to invite her secretary to share her cab. It was not due to callousness, but simply indifference.

37

against appearances are aware bear but contrary despite did even ever filled herself I'm indefinite lives manages nevertheless not nothing of our perfection properly quite repetition same she shield stated tedium that the to Whitehead will with

47

Quite properly, Whitehead stated that even perfection will not bear the tedium of indefinite repetition. I'm aware that our lives are filled with repetition. Nevertheless, she manages, despite appearances to the contrary, to shield herself against the familiar. To her, nothing she did seemed ever the same.

88

a after although an and another around astounded at back bar barman be before brain clipped chose completely corner cut did difficult drink driver elevator entered exactly five fragility fragments frugally glanced glass going goodbye greeting grip has hailed hand handkerchief happened he held her his ignorant in informed interested it latter lobby long me meter might miss neck next Slavic sweet table taken taxi testing the then thoughts through tipped to told took unusual up voice watched walked was what when where window wipe wished without wrapped

177

At five she took the elevator to the lobby. She did not see the other people in the elevator. She walked to the corner and hailed a taxi. She informed the driver in her clipped voice where exactly she wished to be taken. She was completely ignorant of what might be going through his brain . . . she was not interested in his thoughts, in his long Slavic name, or in the back of his neck. She glanced at the meter. She tipped frugally. She entered the bar without greeting me, although it was difficult to miss seeing me. She chose a table next to a window. She ordered one drink then another. She held the glass in a surprisingly strong grip. She was testing the fragility, the perfection of glass, astounded when it shattered in her hand. It was not an unusual occurrence, the barman told me later. She wrapped a handkerchief around her cut palm and watched the barman wipe the table after he had swept up the glass fragments. She swept past me without saying goodbye.

32

a all and as at bar barman certain drinks eyes flourish glasses his I in least mixed of people poured the there time twenty unbroken watched watching were wiped with years yet

42

I watched the barman as he wiped the as yet unbroken glasses and with a certain flourish poured and mixed drinks, all the time watching the people in the bar. There were at least twenty years of watching people in his eyes.

21

and bar black didn't don't drinks entered guys I in jackets know leather ordered remembered the they three were what who

25

The three guys in black leather jackets entered the bar and ordered drinks. I don't remember what they ordered. I didn't know who they were.

77

a about American another apprehensive are asked bar barman being beers black breaking but by capable covered divided do doing fidgeting glad glasses go hands he here himself his holding I'm immense in it it's john kept leather looking me my never not number occur of on one ordered perfection presence public quite round slightly so someone surface telephone that the their them then they they're those thought to unhappy underneath use watched were what would zippers

103

Those immense zippers divided the black leather surface that covered the American perfection underneath. Their hands were quite capable of breaking the glasses they were holding, but it would never occur to them to do so. The barman was unhappy about their being in his bar. He kept fidgeting about, looking slightly apprehensive. They ordered another round of beers. What are they doing in my bar, the barman asked himself. One by one, he watched them go to the john. Then he watched them use the public telephone. They're here to do a number on someone, he thought. I'm glad it's not me.

11

after barman before had left never said seen the them they

11

Never seen them before, said the barman, after they had left.

3

I leather replied

3

Leather, I replied.

4

agreed he leather yeah

4

Yeah, leather, he agreed.

34

a against apartment apartments bulwark city does have her imperfection in intrusion is jacketed leather like many men my of on other particular said say she so subject the this three to what Whitehead

37

This is my apartment, she said to the three leather jacketed men. Her apartment, like so many other apartments, is a bulwark against the intrusion of imperfection. What does Whitehead have to say on this particular subject?

21

body contend has her imperfection it is lips long nose of she tall taste the thin to too walk with yet

39

Yet she has the imperfection of her nose to contend with. It is too long. The imperfection of her lips. Too thin. The imperfection of her body. Too tall. The imperfection of her walk, the imperfection of her taste.

28

all and are brown but couch doorman elevator everyone flaws friends her in jacketed leather men office on overlook prepared quite sitting so soft the these three to

35

But the elevator man, the doorman, everyone in her office, and all her friends are quite prepared to overlook these flaws. So are the three leather jacketed men sitting on the soft brown leather couch.

10

displeasing finds incongruity not of presence she slight the their
10

She finds the slight incongruity of their presence not displeasing.
29

*and bedspread black bright enhance exotic floor foot four furniture
gleaming her is jackets leather Mexican of perfection plant polished
possessions silk she surface the their trousers wearing yellow*
36

Their black leather jackets enhance the perfection of her possessions.
The polished surface of her furniture, the Mexican bedspread, the exotic four foot plant, the gleaming floor, and the bright yellow silk
trousers she is wearing.
39

*a absorbed all and are blows bruised but can fabric faces from get
hands have impassive is jackets knees leather longer look men need
new no not of on reassurance resting the their they three tough
trousers worn young*
56

The three men are no longer young and their jackets are not new.
They have a bruised look from the blows they have absorbed. But the
leather is tough. The men have impassive tough faces, but their hands,
resting on their knees need all the reassurance they can get from the
fabric of their worn jeans.
47

*a also are available by chuck convey described descriptions discard
doorman elevator every far farfetched from furniture have I it just
kind loyalty man managed needs not now of office old on out people
reliability so succession taxi taxis the their then they thrive to trips
who*
62

I have managed so far to convey the reliability and loyalty of the elevator man and the doorman. I have also described a succession of
trips by taxi to and from the office. The descriptions are not farfetched. Taxis thrive on the needs of people, the kind of people who
every now and then discard their old furniture, just chuck it out.
77

*a all and are array arrived bedroom been blank brain breakfast by
can change channels cigarette day designed do everything face faces
firm fixed front fucked furniture had has her how I illuminated imprinted in interiors it large left let's limits men mirror morning much*

newly of on once one other out person pieces place remained room
routine same she smoked sound spotlight succession switch the there
to tossed treasured turn unchanged view voices was were with
117
Everything I once treasured in her place has been tossed out. One
day men arrived with large pieces of furniture and in turn left with
other large pieces of furniture. The view from the front room remained the same. There are, let's face it, limits to how much any one
person can change everything. She fixed her breakfast in a newly
designed kitchen, fucked in a newly designed bedroom, illuminated
by a newly designed array of spotlights. The morning routine remained unchanged. The face in the mirror remained blank. She
smoked a cigarette. Imprinted on her brain were a succession of faces,
interiors, and the sound of voices. All she had to do was to switch
channels.
29
a ability and as available certain communicating did enabled express
having her invite meet men mind on she so speak the them three to
unspoken visit was what without
34
Her ability to speak enabled her to meet the three men and without
having to express what was on her mind, invite them to visit her,
communicating as she did so, a certain availability.
53
a afraid against all Anadelle Anadelle's American Arizona as at been
black book defense did dinky do face Georgina Glow guardian had
have head her in indignation jackets leather librarian like look looked
men not of on perfection read reminded she single the their then
they three to town was who women wore
75
To the three men she looked like Anadelle the librarian in their dinky
town in Arizona. They had been afraid of her. They wore their black
jackets as a defense against women who reminded them of Anadelle
Georgina Glow, the head librarian. Anadelle was the guardian of
American perfection in their town. They did not have to read a single
book, all they had to do was to look at the indignation on Anadelle's
face . . .
9
a how know librarian resembled she that to was
10
How was she to know that she resembled a librarian?

105

a an and any anything apartment avoided balanced being between black blowing bought brain by cab city could cover crash die did disharmonious distance doorman down drop elevator embankment emotion either everything evoke fearful for furiously go good gray hail have he hear her him his if imprinted in into investments it jackets leather light man men might mind morning mumbled new not now objects of office on or overlapped painting pavement perfection plant pleasant plunge rang realism resembled Rosenquist see screwed she stare still stood suddenly that taxi terror the thought three to unaware unpleasant waiting was well were whistle white would wrong York

167

The objects in her apartment were either white or a light gray. In her mind she could see the distance she now would have to cover between her apartment and her office. The thought did not evoke any pleasant or unpleasant emotion. She rang for the elevator. The elevator man avoided her stare. He mumbled good morning. He was fearful that the three men were still in her apartment. She stood on the pavement waiting for the doorman to hail a cab. She could hear him blowing his whistle furiously. The realism of New York City was imprinted on her brain. It overlapped the realism of being screwed by three men in leather jackets. The overlapping was not disharmonious. If anything, it resembled a painting by Rosenquist. A well balanced perfection of terror. She was not unaware that anything might go wrong. The elevator might suddenly plunge down, the taxi might crash into an embankment, her investments might drop, and the plant she bought might suddenly die.

66

a adoration all also an and are be boss coat costume day discreet downpour drink during expensive eyes familiar far filled forsaken god had have her imagination in invited it lift lived loyal might of offer on one only out place raincoat rained rampant ran secretary several since she shoes smiled some sudden the them then those timidly to unexpected up was way with wore would

101

On the day it rained she wore her raincoat. It was an expensive coat. She had several. Her secretary was familiar with all of them. The secretary was also familiar with her shoes and her costumes. The secretary smiled timidly. She was discreet. She was loyal. Only her imagination ran rampant. One day her boss, during one of those sudden and unexpected downpours, would offer her a lift, and then, since she lived in some god forsaken far out of the way place, she might be invited up to have a drink . . . The eyes of the secretary are filled with adoration.

35

a Africa alphabetical bed book could fixed from had hair her lent likely low lying make more morning near not of on out reading recall she sitting someone table the title to was where why

56

She fixed her hair in the morning. From where she was sitting she could make out the title of a book lying on the low table near her her bed. The title was *Alphabetical Africa*. She could not recall reading the book. Someone had lent it to her. More likely someone had forced it on her. Why????

103

a about again all although an and are around as bathroom be bedroom but by can cash casually closet couch dining doorman down drawers eighth evaluate examining expensive fear few floor foot for former four fridge from have her horse husbands if in inside is know leather leave like loyal men might mirrored monogrammed never no not nothing of office on one open opens or out park pass people permitted plant pull reluctant riders ridden room secretary see she squint stroll take that the them themselves there they thick three to towels tropical trying unfamiliar unimpeded view visit wall weekend will window would

171

The three men know nothing about her. They evaluate her by examining the four foot tropical plant, the expensive leather couch, the bedroom and the dining room. They know nothing about the office, or her loyal secretary, or her former husbands, or the people she will visit on the weekend. All they can see is the mirrored wall in the bathroom, and the thick monogrammed towels. They casually open a few closets and pull out a few drawers, but there is no cash around. From the window they have an unimpeded view of the riders in the park. They know the park inside out, although they have never ridden a horse in the park. The view from the eighth floor is unfamiliar to them. They squint, as if trying to see themselves down there. They

would like to take a stroll in the park, but are reluctant to leave, not
wishing to pass the doorman for fear that they might never be permitted in again. One of them opens the fridge . . .

164

*a absence absent acquaintance about again all American among and
any apartment appreciated are as at back barmen be bedroom bedspread been best between bread break bright buffet but by carefully
carrying cheese cleaning clues cold color continuation conspicious
crowd dainty definite discouraging displayed distance don't doorman's drinks elevator erased even evenings everyone's everything examined except firmly floor footprints for forth found freezer friend
fridge furthermore glass gleaming greeting guests had hand have her
holding home how hundred ice in inquisitive inside invited it is know
lack leather least lips little maison man's matter may means men name
neatly never no not nothing nourishment occurred of off offering on
one other others outfit packed party pâté perhaps perplexed platters
present pressing probably prowl reduce remembers scrutinized sealed
searching settle sexual she silver so something soup spends splendidly
table that the their there those three throws toast to tomato totally
triangles twice two uniformed view waiters walking well what white
who will write yearly yellow*

307

They know nothing about her except what is on view. What is on
view is splendidly displayed. It is, furthermore, on view in order to be
appreciated. On the other hand, the interior of the fridge is discouraging. It is not packed. There is a definite lack of nourishment inside that gleaming combination freezer and fridge. They settle for
tomato soup and cheese on white toast. What is not on view is the
party she throws twice yearly. At least one hundred are invited.
Again, everything on view is scrutinized. There are two barmen and
two uniformed waiters offering the guests pâté on dainty triangles of
white American bread. The pâté is *pâté maison*. It is nothing to write
home about. The little triangles of bread are neatly arranged on silver
platters. Nothing but the best. She remembers everyone's name, and
spends all evening walking back and forth in her bright yellow or
orange outfit greeting friends. She believes the bright color will reduce the distance between her and the others, those inquisitive ac-
quaintances who prowl the apartment searching for clues, searching
for something, they probably don't even know what it is . . . perhaps
it is what is absent, that what is not to be found among the crowd
at the buffet table . . . all her guests holding ice cold drinks, but no

one pressing the glass so firmly as to break it. No, that had never occurred . . . Perhaps her guests are perplexed by the absence of any conspicuous sexual clues. But the doorman's lips are sealed. The elevator man's lips are sealed as well. The three men in leather have lips that are by no means sealed, but they are not present. They are absent. Totally absent. No matter how carefully one may examine the bedroom floor, or the bedspread, their footprints have been erased by the cleaning woman.

17

an American and another diary in introduction is great my Saturday simply Sunday the this to weekend

20

This is an introduction to my diary. In the diary the Great American Weekend is simply another Saturday and Sunday.

47

a and apartment are carefully design doing escape expect fighter for George given going hatch he he's how I I'll interior is jet latest me mechanism my navy new now oh on returns said she see smile smiling splendid the to up weekend whose working yes you

55

I expect I'll see you on the weekend, she said to me.

Yes, George and I are going, I said carefully. Smiling.

She returns my smile. How is George?

He's splendid.

Whose apartment is he doing now?

Oh, he's given up interior design. He's working on a new escape hatch for a navy jet fighter.

8

did he I love my place to what

8

I love what he did to my place.

7

it let me must see sometime you

7

You must let me see it sometime.

9

at had I it party seen the thought you

9

I thought you had seen it at the party.

4

didn't invite me you

4

You didn't invite me.

11

an Brazil from I it next oversight return was when year

11

It was an oversight. Next year, when I return from Brazil.

25

believe besides Brazil care couldn't do don't flatly George going he her I in look miserable oh said she's slightest the to told why you

34

She's going to Brazil, I told George.

Don't believe her, he said. Besides, why do you care.

Oh, I couldn't care in the slightest.

I don't believe you, he said flatly. You look miserable.

46

ability about after along another are ask at Brazil car could despite do drives George going have her independence no now one overtaking parkway rear said same seat she sit table Taconic the this thrust to two upon valises was we weekend what why will wishes

66

Now she drives along the Taconic Parkway overtaking one car after another. Her two valises are on the rear seat. Despite her independence, her ability to do what she wishes, this weekend has been thrust upon her. She could have said no. She could have said she was going to Brazil. We will sit at the same table. George will ask her about Brazil. Why Brazil?

73

against and any anyone as at available because bed been besides but by case company desired doesn't dressed elegance else encounter even event familiar flaunt had has have her herself if impeccably in independence invite men mitigated most needed next not of other ours perfection perfumed perhaps pleasurable prefer represented room self-assured she single skin sleep smooth something teeth the their these they this to wanted was weekend were white will would young

95

She has the next room to ours. As if to flaunt her independence she doesn't invite anyone to her room. In any event most of the single young men at this weekend prefer the company of other single young men, but even if this were not the case, even if these self-assured impeccably dressed young men had been available, their elegance, their smooth perfumed skin, their white teeth would have mitigated against a pleasurable encounter in bed, perhaps because they represented the familiar perfection, and in bed something else besides perfection was wanted, needed, desired.

74

a after almost and any apart as aware awed back before below black brand by carpet closed couch did ever familiar fixtures found front furniture had half helpless her horse immobile in interests it jacketed kneeling knelt leather legs lighting men mind new not oblivious of on one other own paintings park perfection place pricks row sat seen she somewhat sucked surroundings the then them their they three took two view volition walls visit

127

Had any of the three black leather jacketed men ever seen her kneeling before? She did not mind kneeling in front of them. She did it of her own volition. She found the experience an interesting one. It took place in her familiar surroundings. On her own carpet. She knelt in front of them as they sat on her brand new leather couch, their legs apart, and sucked their pricks, one after the other, one then two then three. They sat back with half closed eyes, not oblivious of the perfection of her furniture, her lighting fixtures, the paintings on the walls, the view of the horsemen in the park below . . . they sat in a row, immobile, almost helpless, extremely aware and somewhat awed by their surroundings.

43

a all and back blouse but butter can carefully carried dinky drained emotion faint familiar flat from head hear her home I in it librarian men of recollection said she speaking succinctly that the their them three to town unbuttoning voice whatever while

59

I can hear her speaking to them. I can hear her familiar flat brittle voice, a voice that drained all emotion from whatever she said, a voice that carried to the three men the faint recollection of the head librarian in their dinky town back home. But whatever she said, she said it carefully, succinctly, while unbuttoning her blouse.

FIVE POEMS

FRANCO FORTINI

Translated by Michael Hamburger

THE GOVERNOR'S SPEECH

Do you want me to prove by syllogisms
the pitiless strangulation
of fugitive slaves or the malignant charity
of the priests, their vileness?
The almond blossom is over, friendly nature
has made so rich and so melancholy
this majestic mountain range.
Rather see in the bloom of that servant girl
a jet of living blood
her plump arms perceptible to the naked eye
over there, in the castle decorated with vines.
                                    The talk
at supper—I've told you– was all disjointed and jumbled.
But now that the reverberation
slows down and it's growing dark
why waver in the painful study
of that ephemera? Isn't it better
to pretend that nothing happened?
Don't look at those fires on the mountaintop.

SAN MINIATO

I don't know anyone, no one knows me.
If the dead could see they would see like me.
They would hear this howling
of men and women slaughtered
who cannot rest.

Bones and feathers settle in the tar.
Flakes of bark detach themselves from the plane trees.
The leaf goes where it sticks and disintegrates.
I penetrate the evening of churches and of souls,
nothing can harm me any more.
I pass through the abomination
of incense and of wax,
the picture of this moldy vineyard
the odor from a fire of olive boughs,
of laurel boughs
that burn with the litter on the hill.

THE DIFFICULTY AT THE DYE WORKS

To Comrade Wang Tong-kein
secretary of the former Party Committee
the workers at a dye works in Peking
said:
"There was a time when we hated you. But that
which we hated in you
was your errors."

From those words can we gather
what it is that distinguishes
opponents from enemies?

We have enemies.
In them we hate not only their errors
but the bodies that carry them.

And we have opponents too
and we hate the error in them
that has already been in ourselves
or will be.

How happy those Peking workers would be
if they had only opponents.
If they could be humane
towards them and towards themselves
and pitiless only towards error!
How happy we should be
if only enemies faced us.

THE BLACKBIRD

Bird that are saying "rise again,
soul," crying out from the copse
of maple and acorns, blackbird
of bitterness, and from the wine
of violets or from the caves
of alabaster or from feeble crosses
of Avetino,

yes, you are saying, let it drown,
the exhausted mind, the wrinkles
in the spring of youth
that always wells in the wood's midst
where is the paradise of ivy,
where awakening is laughter
and your note does not hurt.

And where everything is as it was,
clear-cut by virtue of hedges
in mirrors of furrows and clouds
to the young man of wax and vehemence
who in the wind heard you praise
the hour of Easter, and saw
the convent up in the blue disappear.

O ridiculous gentle void
called my soul, to rise again,
you know it, is for those who remember nothing.
And instead of what Ireland of the dead
are you telling, of what strange plants
are you stammering, of what limbo are you
the iciest rill.

THE APPARITION

And unnamable man continues to vanish and to appear. As
though on a television screen. You won't hear him howl.
He keeps his hands in the heap of small intestine that
oozes on to his haunches, his corneas peeled.
But you must not describe him.
You must not force a single word.
All remains to be contemplated.
All remains to be done.

SINGING IN THE CLUMP

COLEMAN DOWELL

"Awake/And smell the fragrance of/A June morning/It's past dawn-
ing . . ." Fatty was singing at the top of his falsetto in the tangled
field, hidden by the clump of ivy-hung scrub trees from the gaze of
nearby farmhands. Startled birds, after a time, sang along. The birds
were not startled by his voice in the grove—he was there almost as con-
tinually as they that summer—but by the unfamiliar tune: Fatty was
writing a new song after a week during which he had performed his
latest number, "Who's Venus Compared to You?" to the point where
the birds had come to accept it as the identifying call of his species.
"There's a fatty," they could have said, recognizing the featured
afterbeat. The melodic line of the new song, or call, was long, ascend-
ing, the nightingale's rhapsody inverted. The words, riding the surface of its streamlike flow, were carried far afield.

"Fatty?" asked his sister in the kitchen, pausing at the foot of
the stairs, having wandered down for second breakfast while bed-
ticking spilled airing from upstairs windows and plumped pillows
sat around in chairs like pasty old ladies napping. The mother held
up an assenting forefinger from which dough flaked. The girl panto-
mimed a question— "Where?" "In the clump," said the mother, bright
eyed and waiting as if her daughter's year away at school were expected to imbue her further remarks with pertinency if not wisdom. The girl poured coffee, scrounged a piece of bacon from the

warmer, and sat, forgetful of both, staring vacantly out the window as though smitten blind by the glare of roses. Musingly she said, "That little bitch freak. I could have slapped her." "Don't let your daddy hear you talking like that," said the mother, sinking her fist up to the wristbone in dough. "Huh," went the girl, "did you see *his* face? He would have wrung her cheeks for a penny." Resentment marred her smooth face briefly. "I didn't think *that* would still be going on, at Fatty's age." "Why, yes," said the mother in a reasonable voice, "Yes, it is." She leaned her weight on the imbedded hand, the tendons in the scrawny brown arm standing out. She rested that way for a time, the vacancy of her expression matching her daughter's. The still summer morning transmitted unflawed into the cool kitchen Fatty's song and the accompanying twitter of birds. "It wasn't *her* face he wanted to slap," she said. The girl glared briefly then sighed, dropping her eyes to her mother's hands. "Mama," she said, determinedly amused, "that dough's pulling you in, like quicksand. When they come home and ask where you are, I'll just point to that pile of dough." Fatty's chorus ended; the quiet trembled as though on the point of finding its own voice, then subsided. "Pretty," said the mother, yearning. "Pretty!" mocked the girl, hating herself for hating, "Your two feet sticking out of that dough, pretty!" "Don't be a torment," said the mother. The girl bridled halfheartedly. "Oh, yes, I'm the thorn in your side; always have been, haven't I." "My sides are fine," said the mother smartly, "no thorns that I know about." As Fatty began a new chorus on cue, the girl lifted an ironic eyebrow but her mother headed her off with a request. "Tell me about boarding school," she said, adding, in the girlish tone which never stirred her daughter to confidences as she always hoped it would, "We haven't had a *minute* since you got home. I'm *dying* to hear!" The girl thought, Oh, Mama, don't, but knew she couldn't ever say it aloud, or admit to anyone how much her mother's gushing had always embarrassed her, the same as if her mother were a man. When her mother spoke that way it was as unnatural sounding as Fatty when he aped her, as he frequently did—had done, at least. "Well," she began, thinking, Oh God, this summer; not even one day of it gone. Her mother took a deep breath, thankful for the narrative begun, and attacked the dough with the heels of both hands, her taloned fingers reaching for the puffed-up white hills before them, drawing the hills into the valleys, causing sinkholes to appear in mountains and peaks to rise from craters as she dealt summarily with the one world surely in her grasp.

"Dad-blame it," said the father, on his way to the barn with a broken harness, hearing the beginning notes of another of the expected day-long encores of Fatty's song. Everything seemed to be conspiring to get his goat: the drought, having to take on more hands, now this delay with the broken harness. He didn't know what made him yank on the harness like that; Old Bess hadn't been doing a thing but standing there, head down, waiting to pull the slide to the creek for another load of water. She had yanked back in surprise, feeling his disapproval traveling to her, and their opposing forces had met and clashed at the weakest point and sundered the leather. Anxiety at the sudden parting of the bond between mare and master had caused her bowels to move. It was just then—he snorted in disgust at the memory—that Fatty's words about "the fragrance of a June morning" had exploded the field into back-pounding, foot-stomping anarchy. Even the old hands who ought to know better had gone wild, choking and doubling over. It was their *excess* that bothered the father. He admitted that the situation was good for a laugh: the prissy words and Old Bess's downhome urge. God knew the men laughed with less provocation all the time; it didn't take much to set them off. It was just the feeling that they were letting off steam that had built up in them from some other fire and would have busted if the chance hadn't come along to let it off. It was just the dad-blamed feeling that they were laughing at *him:* nobody had slapped *him* on the back. It was far from the first time that it seemed to him that he was separated from the others by something a man couldn't see. And the times when he tried to get through, with a story, a talltale or a joke, somehow always turned out to be the worst times with the greatest feeling of distance in between. Straddling barbed wire he thought about the time he'd told a storeful of men and boys about the way Fatty got up in the mornings and went straight to the pump organ, in his underwear, and played and sang until he was ordered to get dressed. He told them so that they could see for themselves that he could laugh about his son, too; that having a son like Fatty didn't make him feel like an outsider. But all he'd got for his efforts was the worst kind of snickers. He'd puzzled about it afterward, admittedly a bit sheepishly because of the idea they might have got that he was trying to ally himself against his son, which was not so; he was simply trying to present himself as a balanced man. He wondered if his failure to make his point was due to a wrong choice of word, or words, not that there was such a great choice; in his world, words were like the farm equipment and the people themselves: they had to do extra duty because the supply was limited. Still, reaction was not something you could count on anyway, in man or beast. Old Bess yanking her head, snapping the harness. He'd been party to it, of course, because the first yank had been his. Ah ha, he thought, pushing the pasture gate open, that's it: they'd heard what that little old foreign girl said about Fatty last night. No wonder they were fit to bust. Which told him all he needed to know, because the only one who could have spread the story was the girl's grandfather. His frustration stung like a wasp. He would not be in a position to retaliate until threshing time, and he was not a good bider-of-time. The gate squealed, and he made a note to bring the oilcan back with him. If he forgot, his wife would be after him, saying it set her teeth on edge every time she went through to the pasture. Mountains out of mole-hills, he thought gloomily, entering the tack room and setting to work on the harness. He thought further, cloudily, that molehills produced mountains in country places as regularly as cows calved, but if you followed the mountain to its source you could at least identify the source as a molehill.

Hody and Chigger, on their way to fish and swim in the farthest pond they knew, crouching down the grassy lane so their heads wouldn't show above the runty sumac, stopped at the sound of Fatty's song and straightened up for a minute as if they'd been found out. Hody started to laugh, recognizing the voice. He managed a guf-faw before he stopped, sensing caution in the way Chigger stood, and the need for caution. Chigger had Indian blood that tempered his body like a knifeblade, and some ways he stood and looked you couldn't tell whether the blade was folding or unfolding. Chigger wasn't stronger than anybody else, and he could be licked, except when his Indian blood—"knifeblood," Hody thought of it as—was up. Then nobody could lick him, not grown men or anything. It made him a good friend and a dangerous enemy, and he was Hody's idol, though like everybody else Hody did not know the secret of what it took to rile up Chigger's knifeblood. He had seen men and boys try to get Chigger mad, for the hell of it, without succeeding; then a word, or a look, or nothing, and Chigger was ready to take on bear cats. Seeing the way Chigger stood listening, Hody was certain that his knifeblood was up, and what was more, was aimed against everything and everybody except old Fatty, singing in the clump.

Standing in the lane they could see the clump but not Fatty. The voice shot out of the clump like arrows, sharp and swift; you could almost see the ivy move on the trees as the voice pushed past, nicking the leaves that were in the way. Hody, thinking about Fatty and Chigger and the end of *their* friendship, and wondering how he could stand it if he lost Chigger, felt suddenly pierced with the pinging arrow-words, felt himself bristling with them, porcupine like, standing bleeding in the overgrown lane. He stared at Chigger, wondering if he was bleeding too. Chigger stood turned sideways, his chest like a shield from which the arrows deflected and entered Hody, standing a step behind and to the left of him. Once Hody realized, he took the arrows meekly and let his hide do penance for his mouth's mistake.

She swung on the gate, not counting the *backs*, counting only the *forths: forth* and *forth* and *forth* she swung, imagining the gate was taking her to the moon. She had brought a tree along with her for shade and color in the white journey. Above her the leaves hung motionless, tiny and separate as peepholes punched in a white sky to allow glimpses of the green sky which lay beyond. The tree was in full bloom, but it was easy to imagine the creamy racemes, swinging of their own weight, into clouds, or clusters of air-fruit. For a moment she concentrated on the idea of a forest-sky beyond the white one, and a grassy sun, but before the idea could effect change she rejected it as merely bizarre rather than appealing. She could not allow her need to be on the lam to interfere with the physical setup of the solar system. Someone else, enroute to somewhere out there, flew too close beside her. They, whoever they might be, had a phonograph aboard, and the song repeated and repeated. She thought how difficult it was to find quiet, even in space, but it seemed that, song or no song, she was still to have her noisy guilt to stand between her and the peaceful stars. She thought hopefully, but not quickly enough, that the song was pretty; earlier thoughts caught up with her . . . but thoughts were, after all, the first heavier-than-air craft to fly. She made a mental note of the observation, proving that she could at least keep the rude, clamorous earlier thoughts waiting, then opened the door abruptly, countering remark with remark. Very well. She had not meant to be unkind. As a scientist she merely observed, made observations. Sometimes, out of a sense of social obligation, she observed aloud. When she drew comparisons it was again a social consideration: comparisons are the quickest way to make oneself understood. In her notebook she could have notated it thus, simply:

Fatty $=\,Q$; or, needing words, she could have written, "Fatty resembles that grouping of homo sapiens bearing organs in which are organized large non motile gametes requiring fertilization by smaller motile gametes." But on her grandfather's farm the result of such a precise statement would have been alienation and quite possibly an ego-unsettling paddling, since the purpose of her literal farming-out for the summer was to encourage a more—to use her father's meager word— "normal" way of expressing herself; to, as he had put it to her grandfather, "bring her down to earth, for God's sake." And here she was on her way to the moon because she had expressed herself "normally" about Fatty, to Fatty's parents and Fatty himself and to the sister, with whom she had hoped to be friends. As she had really hoped to be friends with Fatty, too, though perhaps her urge there had not been so altruistic. She had never known anyone like Fatty and had wished to study him, but certainly not to hurt him. And now the summer shot to hell on its second day out because she had thought that *intention* determined a word's weight with regard to its potential to wound. "Hallooooo there," she called, rocket to rocket, hoping to hear an answering voice, one which was reassuringly scientific, unemotional. God knew how long she might have to stay up here, eating locusts.

"ALL the boys have the month of June to unwind in," said the mother. "At least, all the younger ones do. YOU know that." The oven was making its presence known in the kitchen. Flies droned like emery wheels at the windows, a sound hot enough to melt the screens. The sun, in one leap, had made it to the tin roof of the kitchen and curled up there, too comfortable to move on to the other side of the big trees. The daughter pared potatoes and asked questions, sounding as if her year away at school had afflicted her with amnesia for the matters and customs of home. "You don't have to snap," she said mildly, head bent over the sink. The posture caused her still-unfamiliar grown-up face to be cloaked in twin falls of hair and exposed to the mother's prolonged gaze the tender little-girl nape. "Excuse me," said the mother briskly, "It's the heat talking." As her daughter's head swung around she turned somewhat hurriedly back to the biscuit board, leaning into her final attempt to make some meaningful change in the doughy world by stretching its horizons as far as they would go. "Excuse *me*," said the daughter, wondering and touched by something in her mother's tone. "I really had forgotten that." She pondered a moment. "Of course; that's it. Mama, where on earth is Chigger?" She had to repeat the question. "They had a spat," said the mother, and began to hum. "Spat!" said the girl, chagrined and vaguely frightened by some implication now in the room. "Good Lord, you don't spat with your only friend in the world!" "There are worse things, Sis," said the mother and hummed away. After a time the girl said "Mama," sounding as though she had cut herself on the paring knife. The mother thought, She has guessed —she has seen; and knew a weary kind of relief. "I don't know what to do," she began tentatively, "I just don't know." She stopped, then turned swiftly, engaging her daughter's eyes. "I guess you may as hear it, Sis. You're old enough, I guess, to—" She couldn't decide between "forgive" and "understand." The girl said, "*Old* enough?" Her head was reeling as if she were hung by her heels over running water, grabbing at fleeting shapes beneath the surface. "Mama, has Fatty—I mean, is there something else—besides—" Shadowy words glimpsed in medical contexts slid beneath the surface, causing her to shiver in the heated kitchen. She wanted to shout out, suddenly, "What *is* Fatty?" but was terrified that her mother would tell her, using one of those words. The mother felt regret at being so misunderstood, and a lonely satisfaction. She talked rapidly lest her ordinarily sharp-eared daughter hear the difference in her tone and put two and two together, as the mother thought she had done. It was fitting that only Fatty had seen, her summer-singing son, and consoled her with ironic love words, whose irony he trusted her to hear and understand. It was their unspoken secret against the others, against the silence. "His daddy," she began, putting the man in his place; then, to keep him out of the kitchen she said, "*Your* daddy: it's like he'd said to himself that Fatty could just catch up with him, if he wanted to know him, without once stopping to think that *he's* going ahead at the same clip and anyway paying no attention to other turnings along the way and that's to my mind where he's missed out because there's many a turning." I'm getting there, she thought, whether I want to or not. She cut biscuits rapidly, twisting them out of the dough like period marks with which later to punctuate and make separate for herself the autobiographical parts. "Nor will he go back and look. I'm not saying he could find it, it's just he won't try. Once something's mislaid, it's *lost* to him, and of no value; his pride demands that. And still he blames others for the loss, just the way he'd blame the person that found it and claimed it for his own." She thought, That's too close for comfort, and brought it back around to Fatty again with cunning indirection. "He counted too much on Chigger, and when Cigger couldn't do what *he* couldn't do, your daddy blamed him. Still does. But, my gracious, Chigger's finding his own way; how can he point out the way to Fatty, can you tell me that?" "But, Mama, what did Chigger *say*?" asked the girl. "Well—he wanted to grow up—" The mother tried to leave it there, hating to distort, but the girl was persistent: "And Fatty didn't? Is that what he said?" "No," said the mother, "Chigger didn't say that. *I* did. But that's all it is with Fatty. Just—that's all." She loaded biscuits on pans, squatted before the open oven door, letting the heat lap at her as though it were welcome to her. To her relieved-looking daughter she said, willfully autobiographical, "The trouble with some farmers is, they spend too much time with plants," and waited for the heat to draw from her, like sweat, the application of the remark to Fatty. She stood up and closed the oven door gently. "With plants, whatever's planted, that's what comes up. But people aren't like that, Sis." The girl saw the tears in her mother's eyes and was grateful to recall that her mother was not the demonstrative type. She felt that she couldn't bear it if her mother came toward her with open arms, pressing confidences upon her. Whatever was responsible for the tears, the girl knew for certain that it had little to do with Fatty, and she suddenly wanted to think about her brother. It seemed important to do so. The mother, too, discovered that, with all her heartbreak at being alone again within herself, and the brevity of the time when she had not been alone—one brief month in spring, surely her last chance to taste that particular sweetness—for some reason or other she wanted to think about her son. In her covering-up talk about him she had made him sound like an outcast; perhaps, after all, he was. If so, there were two of them now: one to sing and one to listen. She thought: If it turns out that he really is an outcast then I will have to take my turn, singing in the clump. But she did not know how to go on examining what her son was or wasn't. He was too young to be a definite, lasting thing; he was as fluid as water. She thought: Suppose nothing *is* until it's admitted to be; suppose sin without recognition is not sin, nor love, love; suppose that to save my son from being an outcast later on I would have to deny what I had in the two Aprils, and by not admitting what it was—sin and love—it would not have been; then he would not be. Her breast felt empty at the thought. And silent. She listened for Fatty's re-assurance to fill the silence. The song had stopped; the silence rang with the song's cessation. It was the silence she had been listening for since spring, perhaps longer; maybe she had been listening for it

since her son's first word or even before his birth, all through that
other spring following his conception, the spring that found its mirror in this year's April, a long time coming to her hand, so quickly
broken. And now June a summer mirror at the halfway mark, reflecting all before and after: aspiration, need, failure. She had con-
ceived a singer by a singer, out of her heart's hunger, and by the act
had doomed the conception. Starting for the door she thought: No,
not by the act; by the misuse of the boy. Because I feared silence,
the one thing we are born knowing. Life is an attempt to fill it up,
and death when it comes is knowledge of our failure.

Simultaneously the sister thought about how glad she had been,
three years ago, to leave the school where almost daily she was
witness to her brother's humiliation at the hands of the other boys.
She had gone on to the new County High School, relieved and,
with the appearance of Chigger in her brother's life, somewhat forgetful. Or when she remembered, or was recalled by a question
(usually sly; Fatty's name inspired slyness, even in teachers) she
tried smearing on honey by referring to Fatty, airily, as "The Genius"
("The genius on our blighted family tree"), hoping the term would
catch on and become explanatory of Fatty's difference. The term
had caught on, another to be used disparagingly. She went back to
her feeling of relief at leaving the school that also contained Fatty
and his plight, and excused herself for it without apology. Girls had
a hard enough time on their own; a popular brother, even a much
younger brother, was an asset; an unpopular one a barrier to be
overcome. She had, however vicariously, shared his humiliations, and
tried not to dislike him for it. She believed she had managed, but the
distance between the schools had been an additonal safeguard. Without him, she had won the title "Most Popular Girl" two years running. The past year, safely away from his subliminal influence upon
her total image, among people who did not know of his existence,
she had won "Prettiest Girl," though not "Most Popular." Yes, that
was what she was looking for! She thought with a pang, for the first
time, about the dubiety of her new honor: the latter without the
former to strengthen it had an unfortunate aura of emptiness, of
image without content. She pressed bravely on. Without Fatty, the
cross she bore so well, whose overcoming was the proof of her
character (her sweetness, her gallant bearing, her humor) she was out
of context; Fatty was her context. Without him she was seen as merely
pretty. Empty. The sense of his presence stood beside her in the

kitchen like a specter, and then the acute sense of his absence. She had only come home late yesterday; she had not kissed him or petted him nearly enough. She turned to ask her mother to excuse her while she ran to the clump to find Fatty and make up for lost time and saw her mother hurrying across the yard, untying her apron strings clumsily. The sister's legs went suddenly leaden. "It's Fatty," she thought. "Something's happened to him," and she crept across the floor with the blood heavy in her legs giving her the gait of a nightmare or—the thought could not be stopped—of the summer stretching before her.

The boys reached the edge of the foul swamp and saw and heard it pulling for sustenance at the barely moist, teatlike clumps of itself. Hody, anxious to go on proving his courage to Chigger, jumped across the moving green slime to the first clump of grass. There was an easier way, involving logs, but that was for other days. Hody had felt, since the lane and Fatty's song, that the clump had thrown the day out of balance—that it physically outweighed the land over which he walked with Chigger, making their progress as difficult as if their way were all uphill. He had stepped very hard, trying with his weight to push the earth down again and make it level so that he and Chigger would not fall backward and roll like stones into the clump where Fatty sang. Hody saw the swamp as their salvation: crossing it was unpleasant but once it lay between them and Fatty they would be safe. Hody had never been in the clump and did not know why he was afraid of it, unless he was feeling what Chigger was feeling; if he was, the way he had in the lane with the cutting arrow-words, then he was terrified for Chigger. Chigger was in great danger of being pulled back and dragged into the clump. Hody could feel the lure it had for him, like a terribly strong magnet. This galvanized him into furious movement. He hurtled himself forward, over the sucking slime, to the next sun-cracked hillock with the sharp dried grass that cut his legs. Yelling in anger and excitement and pain, he turned to impel Chigger forward with his rage and saw that Chigger stood facing (it was the way Hody saw it, even though the swamp was the muck at the bottom of a basin) *downhill*. As Hody watched, Chigger began to walk away. When he reached the fallen tree without looking back, Hody called out in a flat voice, "Indian." Chigger kept on, mounting the tree as though it were a staircase and descending the other side without slowing his pace. The fallen tree cut him in half; Hody could only see him from the waist up. It was that half-person or child—it looked like both—which Hody tried to reach, not caring if Chigger came back and broke his nose, or pushed him in the nasty, green, sucking slime. "Indian giver," he yelled. Chigger kept going.

She found herself stuck in the ionosphere, an unwilling transmitter of thoughts not recognizably her own. It seemed to her that she was receiving alien thoughts and transmitting them to herself, and eventually that she was originating and transmitting and receiving, an operation whose sterility outlined her plight exactly. She looked longingly back to earth and saw the long mutilated summer stretching over the farms, a corpse of her own making, and she wondered for the first time if perhaps her father was not right about her, if perhaps there were things she did not know, after all. One could not stay wrapped in the cool mantle of science all one's days; one had occasionally to emerge in one's own skin and move about in the world unprotected. The way Fatty did! And take one's knocks, the way Fatty did. Of course, that was the answer, right before her eyes. She and Fatty were really two of a kind; of all those around her this summer, he was the one to understand; to share. She admitted that she was afraid of being called "freak" by those not in her peer group, by inferiors—she thought a moment—and superiors. At home there was a sign on her laboratory door that read THE FREAK, but she had put it there. Fatty would understand! She wondered what she would do if she were forced to live in a place where no one shared her interests, or understood them, or knew about them; a place where she was called "freak" all the time. She knew instantly what she would do. The phonograph had stopped; Fatty had stopped singing. "Oh, no!" she exclaimed. "Fatty, don't!" and climbed off the gate and ran down the road, glad of the chance to get the hell out of that ionosphere; but worried, too.

Bent over the harness in the gloomy tack room, the father thought that it was high time the boy started considering him. That caterwauling in a bunch of trees was something a kid could get away with, but when a boy passed thirteen he was on his way to manhood and had to abide by the rules laid down by men for men. Men didn't sing out like that, unless they were on the way home from the fields, or splashing in a tub where just the family could hear. It occurred to him that maybe Fatty didn't know he was an embarrassment to his father. Not that you could outright say it to the boy, but there were ways. And Fatty could be understanding . . . But what did the boy *do* in that clump of trees, besides sing? What was he *doing* in there, the place snake-infested as could be. It was like the behavior of a stranger, somebody not brought up knowing about the snakes in this part of the country. A man could be hit over the head and not have a case in court, just for making the wrong kind of noise behind a man's back, hissing or rattling. Words. Certain words couldn't be whispered in snake country without making a man uneasy. Sissy. Couldn't whisper that word in snake country. It was hard on you in snake country, harder than almost anywhere else, he imagined. Just to survive in these parts proved you were a man. You came to manhood early through survival alone. No other credentials were necessary; just yourself, walking around. Fatty had earned his right to respect and the father was going to see that he got it, from now on. The two of them together, after all, could present a pretty strong front. That would give the bastards something to contend with. He listened for the reassurance of Fatty's voice. Finding the quiet in its stead, he got up, feeling arthritic. The partly mended harness fell to the floor unnoticed. He thought about the way snakes came from holes in the ground, dropped from trees, slid out of logs where you sat, hissed at you from clumps of ivy at eye level, lay sunning on split-rail fences, chilled your hand in hens' nests, coiled there among the sucked eggs. Snakes and laughers, snickerers and snakes, one as inhuman as the other, lying in wait, confusing a man by stealing his money, trying to steal other things; sucking his eggs or taking it out of his pocket on account of a drought, or sneaking around . . . all were thievery. A man couldn't be a leader like he was meant to be if he had to count his pennies all his life, or snatch eggs still hot from the hen, or keep an eye on the back door, listening for snickers and snakes every step he took. He kicked at the harness on the floor, mistaking it for a black racer, tromped on it until it broke in two places. He hoped Fatty was strong enough to do the same until his father got there.

They converged on the clump in the field. Man and wife noticed many small changes in each other—lined faces, stooped shoulders, sympathy. Chigger and the sister glared at each other; their eyes snapped "Deserter!" The erstwhile scientist, amazed at the assemblage who seemed to be weighing each other on internal machines, stepped into the clump, through the green wall, which shivered shut behind her. Nobody made a move to stop her, or to follow. The polymorphous fears separating them from the arena of the clump like a curtain of fluids had ended the long drought so precipitately that they were foot-mired and could not move.

After a time the girl and Fatty emerged, some distance away, she holding onto his arm while he rubbed the sleep from his eyes. Her voice was reasonable but touched with enough passion to carry to those being left behind.

"We simply can't, you know, people like us. Not when we're a-sleep or anything. We have to keep at it, you see. We can't stop a minute, honestly. Well, that's an expression, but still—" The two children ploughed through the clover, heading for the rocket-gate. They did not turn around, but the girl's voice floated back. " 'De-dication' and such words to one side, the *real reason* we have to keep on is—" The others leaned forward but she whispered, maddeningly, in Fatty's ear, following which she and Fatty laughed in two-part harmony.

She became audible again. "Don't you *know* what we are, Fatty dear?" The others saw him shake his head. This time they took a step forward in unison, leaning and craning for her answer, but the noise they made with their big feet covered her reply and all they got was the maddening signature: the double laugh of the children and one bird call from the clump, a perfect major triad.

TEN ENGLISH POETS

**ANTHONY BARNETT • DAVID CHALONER • JOHN JAMES •
TIM LONGVILLE • DOUGLAS OLIVER • J. H. PRYNNE •
JOHN RILEY • PETER RILEY • IAIN SINCLAIR •
CHRIS TORRANCE**

A selection edited by Andrew Crozier

ANTHONY BARNETT: TWELVE POEMS

1
Mud settles.
I was trying to keep up

to penetrate the locale colours
to affirm day to day
stillness, monotonous ineptness.

But the wind, as I awoke,
blew—
a spruce waved
and just snow dropped off
may morn.

2

The bush is shaped like a cupped hand.
Expansive.
Plenty berries will persist.
For the moment bees begin.
Short nettles grow unseemingly.

3

I am thinking about
catkins developing wind borne seeds
indoors.
Do you think for one moment
they would deliberately allow themsleves to get trapped.
O no. They use the slightest draught.

4

I know this place
so well, I thought.
I was born there, and schooled there.
But matters
about which I know so little
as I went away, go back.

5

Scythe. You implant the long curved blade.
Behind the line of spruce, just now, you see
a girl perambulate. Straw grazes the eyes
there.

6

The wasp
comes in
to settle on the house.

Settle on nothing.
The wasp is beastly afraid.
Mucks about, muck about.
Seems so, not to know its job.

Muck about.

7
What is so strange.
What is the matter.
You are so strange.
You look at me like that.
Fellow-feeling, broken
too near the storage.

8
How you grow.
You are no guest,
no guelder-rose.
Light hardly alters you.
How it lasts for you.
How you go on.
At the salt lick
first how pale you are
how red you are.

9
A light rainfall.
A migratory bird
flies into the night

in a quick curve.
I did not see it.
How you are word blind.
I do not know *why*.

How you recognizably falter over a hyphen.
Think how this began.

Compounded of literal
speech.

10
I wish you would
warm to it,
like the rock face
and the water below,
be not forthright,
not devious,
but the rest.
I am not *wish*ful.
How watery my eyes are.

11
One light stares out,
another back,
a blackletter, unintelligible.

My fingertips dig up your sweet smells.

You hardly know it.
You wheeze a little.

12
Here, roughly,
the wickers.

The size and shape deficient.
But they are built in.
They are serious, at risk.

Far off
(not actually so far)
a couple waving. It burrs.
No, it is the winter wild oat
irresolute at the edge.

DAVID CHALONER: FIVE POEMS

1
technology idles below the window
and something forgotten returns
in the way sounds rise from ground level
through the swift intrusion of diluted air
to whisper the name of their hidden tormentor
forced to compromise at last
even the staircase remains bright
bearing the rise and fall with placid resignation
gathering in the vibrant rays
dispersing them obliquely across the angle
of two legs climbing

2   CAMEO
the radio excuses our dawdling
a plastic alibi protects dreaming statuary
tonight you feel you many never talk again
that sense of self-indulgent excess
the notion strikes you as real
although improper

just because it's late and the lights are turned
off and we're not out
on the streets
being deserted by intention
staring avidly at the huge and godless prickle of stars
at work with the irreconcilable adversary
we are to ourselves

3

      a landslide carries the background from sight
the profile of the journey
is set down gingerly alongside
      the sparsely annotated impression gathered previously
the most open of eyes cast obliquely
as a fleeting moment on the timetable   recounts
     and has you looking up   he sniffs   likes the way
it works   the clarification
his ardour and brish stylish panache
      bending cutting and glueing the cardboard scenery
for the systematic fabrication of a landscape
where we will settle down to solve the logical
     sequence of all that is imposed
on the pattern of so much we have yet to
fully understand
     the openings are within our range
by the time we are prepared and aware that
to go back to our former selves is to remain
     and to advance is to accept what is offered
and the chance to rework destiny with clear-headed
abstraction   our responsibilities variously defined
     we take our differing ways
providing extensions that will later form mere fragments
of a definitive vacillation
     rendering the ensuing happiness unique and misunderstood

4
many a lost day behind these oddments
how two hours are just suddenly not here
any more and the wind doing 200 miles
away exactly what it's doing right outside this window
and pushing reaches you with this information
on several points to be considered
as method both mysterious and compelling
the "no nonsense" approach
is up hill all the way
their peculiarities dance at the edge
costumes streaming along the road
there are alternatives and you propose the first
in the madeira bar 6:30 in the morning
do the dreams ignite as visions peopled with smiles
the warriors of the plain defeated
lights reflected from their blue glass helmets
represent a sign a religious experience
liberation of a moment's doubt
of fabulous purpose closely followed
by contradictions you turn without so much as
a backward glance when all else fails

5   THE CAST IN ORDER OF APPEARANCE
the words interlock
        a mirror gathers them together serenely
he turns and smiles as I fold back the sheets
        she sits on the edge of the unmade bed
marooned
        her language of the big break returns years later
in a fur coat
        smoking french cigarettes
posing by the door
        telling us how boring the whole scene is
the spotlight sweeps away from her face
        as the curtains swoop in

maliciously
      they are unable to reach you
she straightens her dress bending towards me
      to wipe a smudge of lipstick
from the corner of my mouth
      I arrive with the bacon sandwiches
and find you sprawled in the chair
      striking flamboyant lines through the script
I can see where chalk marks have been
      hastily rubbed from the floor
they are exchanging opinions on the rehearsal
      and have missed their cue
it seems quite proper and you dash forward
      with hearty congratulations

JOHN JAMES: TWO POEMS

1   THE DRAGON HOUSE
her bright green leather high-heeled pumps

draws back the curtains to the sun & coffee in bed
on trays with legs this windscreen of a morning
moving with beech & yew a stewpond full of goldfish

I would wish to attend to nothing more than that
which is the measure of a lack of prayer

how could I be able to propose anything other?

the way the ice melts all along your back
that soft declivity near your tail

the sun warms through the glass
we drank last night

little yellow cups of Prunelle Noyer & now
what litters today?
a pile of pastoral trousers & an old straw hat
a pale blue notebook bought in Hannover . . .

discard *The White Stones*
open on the quilt at p. 71
finish the coffee
& sniff the smoky November day

which is thrashing about in the poplars
& looking more like poplars in the wind today
though otherwise the life of plants is not so
powerfully bedraggled here, the garden
ordered as a circulating library
soft romance & too much glare
for my watery eyes.

>   So here we all are
>   & here we all are then
>   like a hardy 70-year-old
>   stripped to the waist
>   all tan & grizzled
>   in the gale

& here is the day with its clouds, a Sunday,
& we're writing & reading & checking our oven controls
& wondering if after lunch to become spectators of the unbeatable
base-line-school-of-old, just-get-it
over-the-net-child-or-you'll-spoil-the-game
Diana versus the locals &
Smarden   Bethersden   Appledore
foreign as white clapboard houses
windmills   a curious zeitgeist never very far away
the clouds are getting up from the west
I think it's going to pour with rain, lunch
can't be very far away either as you have this pain
you think is hunger so you eat, you eat too much
& so you are "in pain again"

>   yellow tomatoes

I particularly like
                    what is
Wendy doing in the orchard? She has cut
either a cauliflower
or a . . . ! ? "your English vegetables are so good, all you need
is to prepare them in an American way . . ." so I duck
out under the eaves again, hunting for postcards
& send one with love to:
                    Master B. MacSweeny,
                    90b The High Street,
                    Barnet,
                    Herts.
                            Now it's the turn of
the shrivelled roses. Luckily
she doesn't have her towalong basket, her gumboots
riding mac & floppy flowered summer hat the brim
held down & tied at the chin with a chiffon scarf
of blue or green, ahhh, quick, shut the curtains!
this continuous sun! O rum
bustuous machine, redolent of Picabia,
his *Parade Amoreuse,* rattle
the rafters, the wall & quietude of Grandmama
Daubeney Russell-Clarke her grey eternal smile
enthralls me working freely in the morning though the
easing of the light is also good before Brittania
pulls down her shades of a wintry evening, yes
the piano please Diana, F minor Prelude pushing it away
like pressing buttons
or small clear bells
that sphere out lighter from themselves
against the indolence of the loggy room

What to those fabulous flying creatures carved & white?

2   PROLEPTIC

some casuist palming a sixpence
or thoughts of the heart of man
which is not as beautiful as a football stadium
or is as beautiful as a football stadium
home fo the married people
you ask how old the captain is
the light in the clouds
bathing the odeon
gives nothing away
the pavements in my part of town are purple & grey
I recline at ease in my armchair
an orgy of barbarism obliges me to write something today
galloping through the neck
inconsequential as water
or *Peter Getting Out of Nick's Pool*
I shall give myself up to art
the preoccupation of dull & stupid women
supine art & supremely useless poetry
which makes me ache with laughter
as quick as a name caught on the breeze
when the sun looks as if it's going to disappear behind
        some clouds
I pick up my cup again & go back down to the kitchen

TIM LONGVILLE: FIVE POEMS
FROM *INTIMATE DISTANCE*

1
The parrot that said
goodbye
to say hallo
I know it is not easy
filling our lives

with otherness
ourselves

2
Absent as moorland much of anybody's life
remains untouched and open—radiant—"we don't look
for big words
but say whatever we have to"

simply where we are
our eyes dazzle and indeed
"your voice I hear in the silence—your smile
I smile" in the opulent depths

of our difference deposits
heart of peat
the spade tongue bites
from which we come up

smoothly breathing out of our own heat
preserved and instant

3
The narrow town the narrow streets the narrow lives
reach to the heart
of greed as a system

—not poetry but propaganda
making distinctions
where none exist?

weed through the paving-stone
the absence of alternatives
dwarfs us

only the lowest level
"character" persists
in which to take an "interest"

"I do not think
of myself
as a devourer"—and to think
you have a choice
in worlds like this:
how do you like *your* life?

invent and omit for greater exactness

no fixed limits

the only road
goes in
and comes back out again

breathing

every revolution always
has just begun

4
Of daring
truth
and consequence

light movement
stone to stone across the brook
the balance is endless

uncertain deftness
heel click hand twitch
make it up

as you go along and get your feet wet
putting the right light note in the wrong place
is an accident

upon the scale of these events in which
the improviser persists
making

his mistakes specific
grace notes
exactly placed

in the light of what comes after this
he is becoming always
something somewhere else

5

Expanse of waves of heat and light
held down to the water's edge
by dark clouds moored to the abbey's ruined arch

in small waves under it the small particulars
the pastimes, forms of sport
aimed towards lightness, weight
in balance by the water's edge

"of the human . . . ."

the exact the inconstant
neither blurred nor fixed
the commonplace intimate distance
your wrist your pulse beneath my finger-tip

shaking with fullness shaken
water in the cup spills light

DOUGLAS OLIVER: THREE POEMS

1   INTROIT TO THE SUICIDE CAVE ORACLE

In what cave in the love of love
does swoftness lie as a
melting wax
        a little lava
which the motive motiveless of oracle
infolds in a rock of memory?

The simplest cave whatsoever
with an inquirer at its entrance
a cast-off coca-cola
        can one
light target
of water in the entrance pitch.

His darkening litter trail is of gratitude also
harm follows steeply he distrusts literacy and also
trusts it more illicitly
        his fiction is of wild-he
although a National Trust owns the mouth
of that earthly swallowing-up.

Moves into a lack of weather often raining
no sun remains interminable a few-volt bulb
of war-time torchbeam
        passes by the wet hundred
grounded helmets tenderly
as a footmarker then lifts to the black front.

The beam is absorbed with laughter
of veils in confusion somberly though
the dust of darkness in progress
        no-one waiting
only attacking the solitary inquiry
descending into the mountain to cut the thinnest figure.

The first question narrows
from walk to stoop to the frontways crawl
to the backways crawl
              wriggling
from the grazed surface underground
like a sheep into soot.

Down there hardly worth-while as himself
to receive a dubiously likely motivated answer
not from the lead sulphide sky
             ore lowers to ground
or does the man seat himself either
getting even in a profound cavern.

Across the night his tongue lash score the limestone
in seconds what the stream of centuries more so
whose direction takes the sediment
             we hear to light
outside this stupid stupid stupid careful questioning
of what no-one can tell what we keep telling all the time.

2   THE HARMLESS BUILDING

A genial imbecility pushes at you;
it wears the cottled smile
of the unachieved, strangling in god-like
episodes. Wasps zig-zag powerlessly down
the focus of your eyes, the road of rooms.
A museum full of buddhas, imitation
koh-i-nohrs quite enough in lighter places,
glint inside Henry Irving's make-up case,
white shoulders of unlabelled
birds, a name, Mercedes McCambridge,
the Italianate fountain incontinent with
happiness, such cratefuls of splendour,
little to recapture, you just

pass through, a tray of gold. Unintelligence
tries to form words for its destiny
of incomprehension, aligned doorways call to
you with sounds nearly like forgive.
Here, unpardoned, you look helplessly for
attendants and are borne through
the middle of this bonaventure, foolish god;
its the dogfish-coloured hearts, the whiff
of formaldahyde, its the
goodwill like yours in the show glass. You serve
the moronic, some creature others
keep in an attic but now has all the
harmlessness it needs, within the laughter
of protected pasts.

3   THE FURNACES
                                        Weak flame zone
still it's soon flame on a gas stove down the city's very
          end a weak resort of the pipe network.   Lead tube
               extending forward has
               a house on its tip
and spits light into a dark kitchen.   In the tile surround
                                   alternative gold circlets
spin. The enclosed cooker harbour burns with gas across water   beneath
          a wide beach, as yet unpopulated.   At
               its extremities an old port
               and the so-called new,
"new" because burning waves make ruins flicker on the sea bottom
                                             So the flame
                         hovering on an invisible
moment of change is the least solitary fact of miles of gas
          sent to houses, waves of heat rolling
               under the tormac and here
                    there are three towns:
the apparent is built on another—the one below uninhabitable
                                   owing to corrupt air

the third is still tawny striations in gas vapour from the
    ground, its children having golden hair
        and clothes of gipsy yellow
           materialising
at the gas flare's fiercest point;   the invisible distance, before
                        such colours, remakes
time in its tremulous millimetres and this middle town
    is being remade in sulphur, leaden pipes
        melt underneath and we are no
        longer masters
even of the miniature furnace on a hairbrained linotype machine.
                      Lead solidifies
into words, apt to quarrel, of all others fit to be assassins.   And each
    house is remade a furnace too   the lights go on
        anxiety gives me again that old heart-
         burn. Leonine children
are in the attic of a house ageing downwards to volatile   corruption.

J. H. PRYNNE: TWO POEMS

1   THE BLADE GIVEN BACK

The price of famine on the inner side goes
down to the spark, with snow crystals
                    in the blood,
washing again, And the lane
    clears, beaten by brush, you
        take the toprail
    and push hard, so
           that it opens too
for shale and scree; the mat now in the hotel
foyer grained with ant love. He smiles with
shadow within like a case of mica grips:
there is rage in the lace he calls for and
      gets, out, you go
           down to the sparking

river bed, road spilled with oil
                                flag out
           angered with the shadow driven up.

Too far
          but the iris clouds over to the bank and
we are starving like the man who says right
form and means no less, the rain is
                    from the plain tonight
                                Blood's up, the
          welkin diverges from that
                              makes a dough of
                    failed manners oh please
                    why don't you settle the
          first leaf on the counter, the book by the clock.
The stair goes box by box she stands
                    by the kerb three inches the
                                rest
          is bronchial collapse. The hotel is
                    the black phosphorescent price
of oranges today at the ready, frothing with skin.
Up the metal staircase at the back of this store
I struggle with cautery
                         holding the broom in the
                    stall forward, how the
          year rides to a stop
                              by the orthoclase.

And we are burned out with hunger reversed
again holding, being held
                         as the snow cruises
               to the junctions of recall in the place to stay
                    to put your feet up and be calm
          shielded by the mantle of fields
                                        green
                    and spoken of, coming down.
The hotel lights up on the first floor
                              it gets

> late, veined with inner
>> stair and counter-stair
>>> it makes a war
>> with smoke on the wall:
> the day is lost in greed. Oh rest your head.

2   AGAIN IN THE BLACK CLOUD

>> Shouts rise again from the water
> surface and flacks of cloud skim over
>> to storm-light, going up in the stem.
>>> Falling loose with a grateful hold
>> of the sounds towards purple, the white bees
> swarm out from the open voice gap. Such "treasure":
>> the cells of the child line run back
>>> through hope to the cause of it; the hour
> is crazed by fracture. Who can see what he loves,
>> again or before, as the injury shears
>>> past the curve of recall, the field
>> double-valued at the divine point

>>>>> Air to blood
>> are the two signs, flushed with the sound:
>> (a) "tended to refrain from aimless wandering"
>> (b) "experienced less dizziness"
>> (c) "learned to smile a little"
>> (d) "said they felt better and some indeed
>>> seemed happier"—out in the
>>>> snow-fields the aimless beasts
> mean what they do, so completely the shout
>> is dichroic in gratitude,
>>> half-silvered, the
>>> gain control set for "rescue" at
> negative echo line. The clouds now "no longer
> giving light but full of it," the entry condition a daze
>> tending to mark zero. Shouting and

laughing and intense felicity given over, rises
    under the hill as *tinnitus aurium*, hears the
        child her blue
        coat! his new
        shoes and boat!
    Round and round there is descent through
the leader stroke, flashes of light over slopes, fear
      grips the optic muscle. Damage makes perfect:

"reduced cerebral blood flow and oxygen utilization
are minifested by an increase in slow frequency waves,
a decrease in alpha-wave activity, an increase in
beta-waves, the appearance of paroxysinal potentials."

        And constantly the
    child line dips into sleep, the
more than countably infinite hierarchy of
      higher degree causality conditions
setting the reverse signs of memory and dream.
    "Totally confused most of the time"—is
        the spending of gain
        or damage mended
        and ended, aged, the
        shouts in the rain: in
        to the way out

Run at 40° to the light cones, this cross-
      matching of impaired attention
feels wet streaking down the tree bark,
    a pure joy at a feeble joke.

JOHN RILEY: FROM *CZARGARD*

to get to know the flight of birds, blossoming
of lilac-bush tipped wtih white flame
see the movement of the wind and try
to reassemble quietness from the creakings of the house at
                night, night
when the blood-red sun leaves the room I'd have written a lot
having lots of thoughts and memories of lots of people
in a book of hours, meanings, hierarchies
an Easter greeting always, uncertainties
of private death dispelled, carried closely, nourished
and protected till the time for it and the Poet
subsumed in the poet
                blue
flowers yellow flowers a garden a dog a stick
and courage
            but God decided differently
strangely unrecognisable almost beyond
where we've been the ferns, far plants, anachronisms
rampant, uncoil, sticky and rain hours on end
this garden, prehistoric landscape
                  dirty public wandering
        to know
all cities to have heard and distinguished the cries
that women make and men in pleasure, in pain
the future stretched out as the past in faces
the god of grace floats high up over the cloud formation
hymns raised and lowered, seemingly not
getting any place, the common god
                  what the sea
has to say, what we:after the blizzard they
jumped on sailors to get them in their coffins the schoolmaster
"consulted the elements" both flags we wave
in view, in view of, somewhat gaily : enough greenery
to get lost in temporarily
              reaching out, driven
from pillar to post of millenia blood

thickens, thins
          to get to know
the flight of angels "I have not loved
my contemporaries, I've loved their beauty"
"and pitied myself improperly" *cette pourriture*
I think I hear there the whine of receding light
more than in most
           not much
jasmine scent from the islands
the stink of colossal crime
              still on West Europe

•

delicate the wind through silken corn
a life without compromise
hills over hills unseen the sighing of the wind
weighty in the palm
            wisdom hovers, unheld
tangible, almost, between sense and idea
the cupped hands
          to get to know

and I could not help thinking of the wonders of the brain
that hears that music
the soft moths the soft hills the soft nights the soft breezes
of Asia .
and the music? gone, gone, but here and the form :
except, save (save) in the music of the line it is not, that's
the trick, mind
stumbles at that, not imitating
nature but man's art we heard
a priest chant vespers to an empty church (save
for us, spectators) God
in the City . the brain sticks . proposes
formulations :
           a city
           of squatters, drum

        of the dancing bear at morning, past noon
        both man and bear asleep in ruins, the
            bear's paw
        delicate . easy
            a formulation

dome after dome and dome within dome
was . is . the caves within made
no space made all space having
rhythm and line and necessity
and duty perhaps in the poem one recites by heart
even to no auditors but beauty

a paradox in the very soft breezes
not apparent   for all
that one lives
        and is grateful
for all that without which
        and in spite of
in such plenitude the music
        comes of itself, were we
able .
        how make you hear is to say
how shall I hear . how shall I hear ? say it or how
hear exactly what was heard
            in the ruins
till the time
        or this :

there is a flower
whose colour I cannot see
of pervasive scent
        the name
of the end of all things, in all things .

        the poem . the City .

        a flight .

PETER RILEY: FROM *MARINE LIFE*

1

paled on matchless retract he has
fallen away from her to a valley
heavy with crosses who was so
trusted, and now estranged gives
birth to his mother on the distant couch
so as you'd harly notice, purple
flowers beside him nodding on their
stems as the world would have it so;
what state, in what power he can be
nothing he does not know, dismembered
by lotus ants for the sake of mere
context breaks into green cleft and
occluded wavelength he thought he
wanted this pre-human clarity—

2

to the left, flint / turn /
and to the left, flint.
For the image-box was on the never and once
alone it is night; the earth indicates
its preference for the lost and faithful
while he shrugged out of the light, his
cowboy sabbath in ruins and the cold lizard
deafens at his feet; this venture was
into her eyes he is frightened to look
and the rest of his edge-walk is there
before him, in that are kept, thickening
to cloudy blue beyond the fork. No more
decisions, no more talk. The fault is open:
a razor-blade straight down the middle-

3

ground, and the stream is not clear
and the notch in the skyline fills
in: our daily fuse-box, half

asleep (forgive us) our daily refusal.
And lights enter the bay tonight as a signal
long attended, moontrack vibrating on the
stave a choirboy's cue an iron rod
emerging through branches as a wasp falls
disbanded through the black air, the youth that
emerges in the middle of a life has no name
and intends no harm but it is too late: the sides
touch, reciprocal inhibition explodes, he floats
howling out of the window curves over the hill and
wakes up every sleeping vole on the island,

4

exploding like crackers in his wake, christmas token
at the cottage door for the map is mapped for the victim
but this is the other, who owns nothing, intends
no harm and coils away into genital mist when the
receptive field is out. The nerve is a silent
house and this is the hole where the stone used to be.
And he at his chair and the house and the wish
in its rusty trap, his next face is lithographed
onto green the hand that takes it from him
at the night entrance. His offer calculates while he
dozes. His ignorance falters, flutters in the
elements and settles on someone's shoulder at
last. Damage laid into the distant
future the hypothesis grinds on

5

bedrock, sparked.
A nightchild came shout-
ing at six the imp-
ending reversals:
hedges aflame with
desire come together
at the edge of wish on the
emptiest page forever.
Take it in the
yellow cup reluctant
as normal, for the

landlords can work
this round to their own
promissary lamp

6

while still the ball floats in the air and this
is precisely that point at which the wine
is strongest and he walks into the howl itself
thinking something needs to be done with these
stacks of surplus affection piled open on his
acquaintance with the world—mother sends him out
for fish and chips for dinner once too often, this
mother he had made, and now he curves
in the blackened sky and hill
a danger to everyone. It is the aftermath
beyond electric presence he inhabits, engaged
in transfer to a point of arched diffusion where
the rest is mere adjustment, calling
negative energy to a compacted bolt aimed at
the roofline, not an inch to spare not a pleading vole
and not for the world will he forget

7

to keep steady and sight
the farm on the cliff
created as it is in space
as the third space between us
full of coin, the unsold fruit
we follow with our eyes
all the way to the boiler room.
In that articulated due the house is
vacuumed now, light burns
blueish in the fields around
hazy with lost fur
discarded fuse-wire
cancelled trope
prize virgin forehead
undisclosed.

IAIN SINCLAIR: FROM *SUICIDE-BRIGADE*

FOR PEACHEY, THE EXECUTIONER

Peachey, the hit man,
shifts into pamphlets

a ring of mountains about him

his head-world so heavy
(arm bends)
falls through
the spatulate bones of his hand

an x-ray delicacy

like the braiding on the Hussar's tunic
worn aloud

bowel movements were
the only clock he could trust
& ran progressively slower
as his diet thinned
to goat's milk & diabetic chocolate
suffered the hammer
of phenylethylamine migraines

sponsored by the Taxicab Menswear Mafia
this stick wielder
alludes to arcane practices
is reprinted in Regents Street
overheated
obeys the bugle

a violent trailer
recling & burning between the skin layers
despairing Optographer

●

Peachey had studied the Coffin Texts
been early upon the Mountain
chanted the HYMN TO OSIRIS, for his revival

AH. HELPLESS ONE.
ASLEEP WHERE I HAVE FOUND YOU
LYING UPON ONE SIDE
GREAT LISTLESS ONE
WHOSE NAME CANNOT BE WRITTEN
LET ME LIFT YOUR HEART
YOUR BONES I WILL KNOT TOGETHER
AN END TO WOES
AN END TO SLEEP'S HEAVINESS
LIFE'S FLAME CLIMS THROUGH YOUR FEET
MOISTURE MOUNTS WITH YOUR SPIRIT
I HAVE KINDLED YOU
LIVE GREAT ONE
LET THE SLEEPER RISE
IT SHALL BE MY HOUSE THAT AVENGES YOU
HORUS WILL AVENGE YOU
THOTH SHALL PROTECT YOU
YOUR POWERS WILL AGAIN BE VISIBLE IN THE SKIES
YOU WILL CAUSE HAVOC AMONG THE GODS
YOUR FATHER JOINS ME
HE CALL OUT " COME "
LIVE NAMELESS ONE
LET THE SLEEPER RISE FROM HIS CHAMBER
TAKE UP AGAIN THE BULL'S PROUD HELMET

it could not rest there; Hand praised him
Hyle was not slow in honouring him with gifts
the Old Ones were reverenced, the drum
was made moist with the blood of virgins

at the Double R steps forth Atum
creator of the eldest gods,
malachite green master of the fires
who moves through the space
between two serpentine circles, turning

he also was Peachey's familiar
steps forth in the smokelight, announcing

I AM ATUM, CREATOR OF THE ELDEST GODS
I AM HE WHO GAVE BIRTH TO SHU
I AM THE GREAT HE-SHE
I AM HE WHO DID WHAT SEEMED GOOD TO HIM
I TOOK MY SPACE IN THE PLACE OF MY WILL
MINE IS THE SPACE OF THOSE WHO MOVE
LIKE THOSE TWO SERPENTINE CIRCLES, TURNING

Peachey sweats in malarial excitement;
his confession, the inaccurate
study of the texts, the awkward translations,
sees Hand as Atum, wishes to raise his spirits
miscalculated miles & centuries
released the half-animate flood of demons
the cat-headed boygirls
                    the storm clouds
cumulonimbus over the Chair of Idris
frowns in horror as they drift east
to the pinnacles of the city
                    to Tower Hill
the unsleeping eye of the cauldron

Atum speaks plague on the followers of Peachey

on the Wilsons, Sprague de Campe, Hesse,
the Blakean publicists, the boudoir astrologers,
"the Taozer babbling of the Elixir," Amis,
Gog garglers, Ripper tourists, transvestite druids,
zoo builders, Campden Hill tantriks, Avebury
photographers, stone thieves

may locusts fall on all their heads

(about Powys, he reserved judgement)

horrible things, he whispered, in revenge
for the planners of Golgonooza

(Hawksmoor, he excepted)

thus spoken, it became

CHRIS TORRANCE: THREE POEMS

1   ROCK CRAZY

for Phil & Pat Maillard

  elixir
intercepted at the mailbox
as hauling big bike in direction Glyn Neath
early white frost
gone by the time I attained the hilltop
full ahead up & down through the
cool valley airs
dusky sun brimming up
smoke hooks bent over the valley

wheels tip me down the billow-browed hill
into the grimy town, where everyone has a
friendly word of greeting, asking after Val

& with the 3 day week, & trouble in the coal
the valleys are quieter   "I feel like a beggar"
said a female person interviewed in the dole queue

& look out
for the glacial damming moraines at Clyne & Tonna
that created lakes in ice ages gone by

ochrous-stained tumbled mesas, treeless slacked plains
of the modern desert lands behind Swansea

reck-crazy, my head full of
schists & quartzes, clustered marbly stuffs
of conglomerates, rocks in my pocket

a pied wagtail picking over
muddy-puddles verges at Pontneathvaughan
the giant road on stilts, great-wheeled yellow plant
low of an animal from farmers yard
squeezed in between the higway & the Angel

have had this road march across their backyard
without the evidential logic to resist
aquired purchase

on this & these I reflect
as I leap back up the hill
with paraffin   & hammer & nails
to help build our new fence
the brakes are failing in the dips
I must see to them again

2   MERCURIAL MESSENGER

for Jade & Denise

of Symonds Harvest Vat Cider, 38 ounces
the eggs are washed
Mrs. Brent picks armfuls of runner beans
tribute, perhaps, to

this ability of the S. Wales valleys
up to the Brecon scarp, to trap
the warm continental airs

      the young rams
run at each other
in mutual butting contests
it is a kind of language
the cider is innocent of malice
friendly as the sward
the rams butt on
while the dams nudge by, indifferently,
trailed by their grown lambs

      the Nep is not 'nip
'tho eats may conceivably enjoy it
stretched out at their leisure
while the coals die

      the guitar
raps
the libidinous beetles
tick anxiously in
the ancient wood
the whole earth breathes a sigh
& cracks, the dry explosive
of inert ripeness
& a drowsy wasp flies
onto a plum, & others join, & swarm,
picking audibly
& the ivy buds' lime-green
foretells blossom in
"St Luke's Little Summer"

3   THE OLD WIVES SUMMER

Some sigh of Earth fecundity, relinquishing
a balance of sun energy, that had been brought in, to
soil & sinew, thew of oak releasing first
clattering brown leaves, distorted planes of trackways,
flat spiderwebs glistening in the mossy dew
corn moon stopped full on the horizon
the world stood on its end forever, equinox,
the craw stands still, mutely gaping
cold bright flowers as yet unseared
love has to be learnt all over again
so the bursts of evidence, climax of arrival
warm up a roomful of strangers
will they sustain an enfoldment? together,
opening up the hopefully uncensored self to the present
the fallible, living trace that is us in the world

SELECT BIBLIOGRAPHY

ANTHONY BARNETT. *A Marriage* (1968); *Poems for the Daughter of Lievens* (1971); *Poem about Music* (Burning Deck, 1974); *Blood Flow* (Nothing Doing, 1975).

DAVID CHALONER. *Dark Pages / Slow Turns / Brief Salves* (Ferry Press, 1969); *Year of Meteors* (Arc Press, 1972); *Chocolate Sauce* (Ferry Press, 1973); *Over the Hill* (Big Venus, 1975).

JOHN JAMES. *Mmm ... Ah Yes* (Ferry Press, 1967); *The Welsh Poems* (Grosseteste Press, 1967); *Trägheit* (R Books, 1968); *The Small Henderson Room* (Ferry Press, 1969); *In One Side & Out the Other*, with Andrew Crozier and Tom Phillips (Ferry Press, 1971); *Letters from Sarah* (Street Editions, 1973); *Striking the Pavilion of Zero* (Ian McKelvie, 1975).

TIM LONGVILLE. *Familiarities* (Grosseteste Press, 1967); *Pigs with Wings* (Grosseteste Press, 1970); *Spectacles Testicles Wallet & Watch* (Grosseteste Review Books, 1975).

DOUGLAS OLIVER *Oppo Hectic* (Ferry Press, 1969); *The Harmless Building*, a novel (Ferry Press & Grosseteste Review Books, 1973); *In the Cave of Suicession* (Street Editions, 1974).

J. H. PRYNNE. *Kitchen Poems* (Cape-Goliard, 1968); *The White Stones* (Grosseteste Press, 1969); *Brass* (Ferry Press, 1971); *Into the Day* (1972); *A Night Square* (Albion Village Press, 1973); *Wound Response* (Street Editions, 1974).

JOHN RILEY. *Ancient and Modern* (Grosseteste Press, 1967); *What Reason Was* (Grosseteste Press, 1970); *Correspondences*, prose (The Human Constitutions, 1970); *Ways of Approaching* (Grosseteste Reveiw Books, 1973).

PETER RILEY. *Love-Strife Machine* (Ferry Press, 1969); *The Canterbury Experimental Weekend* (Arc Press, 1971); *The Whole Band* (Sesheta Press, 1972); *Strange Family* (Burning Deck, 1973); *The Linear Journal* (Grosseteste Review Books, 1973).

IAIN SINCLAIR. *Muscat's Würm* (Albion Village Press, 1972); *Birth Rug* (Albion Village Press, 1973).

CHRIS TORRANCE. *Green Orange Purple Red* (Ferry Press, 1968); *Aries under Saturn & Beyond* (Ferry Press, 1969); *Acrospirical Meanderings in a Tongue of the Time* (Albion Village Press, 1973).

GREEN KNOWLEDGE

JAMES PURDY

1   Choristers

Black swans have strange histories, they dream backwards. Certain trees have a shade so dangerous merely to sleep under them causes excruciating headaches.

The frogs have slept on the nightclothes of a prince.

All frogs know this: the prince is deadly white with fear, he has wandered all night through a path bordering marshes. Terrible wings brushed him, but the frogs' voices struck lead fear into his heaving chest. They told all things to his delicate mind: past, present, to-come. The frogs know all, *crug, crog, gork*. The prince went ashen, but the frogs only ceased when an owl flew over their choir: *Die, slimy prophets!*

Crug, crog, gork.

Immediately his horse arrived he rode off like hot lightning streaks in July, but the sound of the frogs pursued the prince even as he lay in his starched heavy sheets with the canopy of a field bed over him. The lady of the chamber took his pulse, she put her wig to his heart and listened, then summoned the doctors from miles off, a council was held, and all agreed: *He has heard the night frogs tell all knowledge, he will never be well again, he will keep pale and have fits because no man can live with the knowledge they have revealed to him. Therefore, let him have the cordials of the forest which assuage in part pain, let no woman enjoy his body, his supper must*

*must be light and taken alone. Permit the owl of the upper forest to
accompany him at all times, or a raven and two crows. He must have
no human associations other than serving people. Keep the lights low,
no sunshine after noon, let him have his sun in wines.*

You too are in deep disgrace for you have not learned the tongue
that frogs speak as you wander now into the dark wood and listen to
their voices. The crow was sleeping but the voice of ten frogs warned
you, yet you were unresponsive because the winter before your *Gram-
mar of Frogs* lay unopened. Had you turned only two pages you
would have understood what they told you:

*Go to the northwest corner where the moon is new, wait till the
the first quarter, then full, and after stripping immerse yourself in
the thickest mud, hold an alder leaf well over your groin, and even
though you have not mastered their green language you may understand two words: SHED BLOOD.*

2   Ball

From the cliff, the crag, and the jagged side, they throw a ball and
catch a ball, no mitt no glove no mask no bat, those are the boys who
play with their bare naked hands, ball.

And throwing so high it becomes all at once as silver as stars, it's
the ball, the ball the flying ball from the hands of the boys on the
summer strand.

*How do you do? says the preacher's wife, how are you and the
girls and the boys and how is the little dog that barks to the breeze?
How are your children and how are their elders, and who is the man
with the hat so high a bird mistook it for a fresh-built nest? How
are your mother and father and sons and the pig that oinks in the
sun?*

Is it a balloon that is floating so high in the air? It's the ball of the
boys that has gone up for a spin as they cry *Catch it nakedhanded
catch it low, one for the money, two for the* . . .

The ball of the boys on the summer strand caught with such
ease with naked hands.

But then to their sorrow they threw it so high it never came down. Downcast and glum, they sat on the strand without mitt glove bat or mask, no ball to fly at them now lost in the wind and the air, and in despair they pulled off their duds and jumped so high they appeared all at once to join every ball long vanished in air.

PARCEL OF WRISTS

STEVE KATZ

In this morning's mail I received a parcel postmarked from Irondale, Tennessee. It was wrapped in heavy, glazed brown paper, like thick butcher paper. The box was of even dimensions, two feet high, two feet deep, three feet long, and it was packed from top to bottom with human wrists.

The wrists were clean and odorless. They had been prepared so neatly, without a trace of torn flesh, that it occurred to me they might never have been attached to hand or forearm. I held one for a moment in the palm of my hand, a small one that might have belonged to a child or a frail girl. It seemed to flex itself there slightly, perhaps in reaction to the warmth of my hand, as if the person to whom the wrist could have belonged were just beginning to wake up. I put the wrist back in the box, closed it, and went downstairs to the luncheonette to get some breakfast and mull over the strange detour my life had taken as a result of my opening the morning mail.

For breakfast I had a toasted bagel with what in New York City they call a "shmear" of cream cheese, a glass of fresh orange juice, and a cup of coffee, regular. I kept repeating to myself the phrase, "parcel of wrists." I could say it rapidly ten times, without a slip. I also said "box of wrists," "carton of wrists," "package of wrists," "shipment of wrists," "bundle of wrists." I am often prone to dis-

tractions. I sometimes read 20 books at a time. I leave them at different locations in my apartment so that I have something to read wherever I pause. I don't concentrate. I don't usually focus well. What I noticed at this moment, however, was that I was absolutely locked in on the problem of "wrist." The word kept firing in my mind like a spark plug. I had been instantaneously and profoundly affected, and I realized that before I could return my life to normal I would have to find the answer to the question of the wrists. I decided to go to Irondale, Tennessee.

I invested first in twenty-five pounds of topsoil, and buried each of the wrists in a flowerpot. There were forty-three pots in all. That I had been sent an odd number made the whole matter seem even more curious. The pots took up a good third of one room of my small two-room apartment; in fact, it had become so crowded in my home that I was glad for the opportunity to get away for a while, out into the country. I tore the return address and postmark off the wrapping paper. C. Routs, Irondale, Tennessee, was the return address, printed rather carefully. I packed a change of clothes, grabbed my sheepskin coat, and left. It was October. The leaves were probably turning. It always seems to me one of the unaccountable luxuries of this hideous second half of our century to be able to take trips on one's unemployment compensation.

I hitched to Washington, D.C., looked around for half a day, and was happy to leave. I took the Greyhound to Nashville, Tennessee. I picked Nashville even though I have never looked at a map of Tennessee, and have no idea what's close to Irondale; but what other alternatives were there? I just couldn't conceive of myself in Knoxville, and Memphis had the sound of a place to raise a family, whereas Nashville seems like a place you can go to, look around at it, and leave again. Until recently I never had much love for country music, but I thought it would be delightful to step off the bus into the heart of the country sound. Not so. Not a murmur of it. A dreary bus station. Blue walls. Years of piss stench. Drunks prodded by police in starched uniforms. I consulted a map under a piece of dirty glass on the wall.

"Irondale?" said the man at the ticket window. "Now you've got a problem there." He looked me over once and then went back to studying his tally sheet.

"I need a ticket to Irondale, Tennessee," I repeated.

The man put down his pencil, and smiled, and scratched his nose, and shook his head, and looked at me. "There is no such place as Irondale, Tennessee."

His accent made me realize I was in the South. I hadn't been thinking about going South, what that meant. The map in the bus station showed Tennessee to be just north of Mississippi, Alabama, and Georgia; what most New Yorkers assume is enemy territory. There was no Irondale, Tennessee, on the map. I didn't know what my next move would be. Generous hospitality and sheer brutality were the two polarities I had stored among my Northern preconceptions of the South. I wanted to make no friends and intimidate no one: utter neutrality was my goal. For that reason I went to a barber shop as soon as I left the bus station, and since that shave I have not grown back my beard.

Vincent D'Ambrogio was the barber's name. It was strange to meet an Italian with a Nashville accent. "You're 'bout number three fer the day."

"Number three what?"

"Number three longhair I clipped. They all come to Nashville to git their hairs clipped."

"Say," I asked, after a pause. "Did you ever hear of Irondale, Tennessee?"

Without hesitation the barber said he had.

"Where is it?" I asked.

"It's in West Virginia. Irondale, West Virginia."

The postmark on the wrapper clearly indicated Irondale, Tennessee. I wasn't about to go to West Virginia. I stopped at a filling station before I found myself a room, to get a Tennessee road map. The attendant had a St. Louis station on full blast, Johnny Paycheck singing:

> There are things to do in Knoxville
> There are things to do in Nashville
> And Rock City is a place you ought to see;
> But if you want to visit my town
> You wont find it on the road map,
> I can't say much for Heartbreak, Tennessee.

"Yew want to buy that Mustang sits out there?" the attendant asked, pointing at a yellow car. "It's a running machine."

"No."

"Don't have a car, do yer?"

"No."

"You sure could use that Mustang."

As soon as I hit my bed I fell asleep, with the map of Tennessee unfolded on my face. When I woke up there was still no Irondale on the map, though I did find an Iron Hill, west of Nashville, and Iron City, southwest, on the Alabama border. I decided to go to Iron Hill first.

"You don't want to go there. Ain't nothin' there." The ticket a-gent at the wicket of the Louisville and Nashville line was myopic and leaned far over his counter to try to see me. "Passenger train goes through but once a day on the way to Blondy and Hohenwald."

"That's where I'm goin." I noticed I was starting to pick up the accent.

"Well go ahead, then; but you're goin' nowhere." He leaned back in his seat, fiddled with some papers, and in a few moments handed me a ticket, a long, elaborately franked piece of paper that guaranteed my transportation the forty miles from Nashville to Iron Hill.

He was right. There was nothing at Iron Hill. It was a water stop. Just a tower. No buildings. An unimpressive hill with some sparse growth and a rusty outcropping of rock that probably gave the place its name. I climbed to the top of it. The land flattened out to the west, and was dotted with sharecroppers' shacks. Cotton country. It was hazy and warm and I was sweating. I didn't know when another train was coming through. I sat down under an old pawpaw and watched the leaves fall around me. Wild peanuts were dying on the hillside. I guess I dozed off because the next thing I rembmber is the sound of giggling kids and the pressure of some small hands on my shoulders. Three of them, waking me up; a boy and twin girls. I don't remember their names any more.

"You want to come home with me?" asks the little boy.

I look up and down the railroad track. There is no sign of a train. "Do you know when the next train comes through for Nashville?"

"When you hear a whistle, that's a train," says one little girl, and her twin sister cups her hands over her mouth and whistles a long, mournful tone, that if I were not observing her do it I would think the train was already upon us.

They said nothing more, but silently led me through the woods for about two miles into a complex of buildings like a small factory complex from the turn of the century, built of bricks and wood. The children disappeared behind some buildings and left me there in sort of the center of things. People appeared in windows, on porches, from around corners. They had stopped their business to look at me. None of them was armed. I wasn't afraid.

I realized I had been led into the heart of a flourishing commune. Everyone looked extraordinarily healthy. The women's faces shined under their bandannas, their breasts pushed out around the bibs of their overalls. The men were all bearded, longhaired, and vigorous, and made me feel strange in my new state of hairlessness. The kids who led me here had taken off all their clothes and were hiding behind some grown-ups. A short, robust man, wearing a railroader's hat and carrying a clipboard under his arm stepped off the porch of the main building and approached me. His face was red under his beard. He was all business. I was smiling, but he wasn't.

"If you want to stay, you'll have to work. Your first twenty hours a week give you the privileges of room and board. After that you get credit at the commissary." He pointed at a small wooden building I guessed was the commissary. "My name is Lith. You'll have to accept the name we give you. We don't allow you to keep your old name while you're here. What is your old name?"

"Steve," I said.

"We'll choose a new one for you. You can stay in that building over there."

I went to the building I was assigned. It was late, and I wasn't sure, anyway, I could find my way back to the railroad tracks that evening. I was curious about the name they would assign me. The wooden building was an old sawmill. It was spotless, not a trace of sawdust. I doubt that the equipment had ever been used. It was that elegant, turn of the century, cast-iron machinery: big heavy cogwheels, counterweights, belt drives, stiff, old leather belts, all of it rusted but ready to go just the same. I loved the look of it. The big, circular steel blade of the buzz saw attracted me especially. Though I have no doubt it was from the same era as the rest of the equipment, there wasn't a spot of rust on it. It had the perfect, bluish glint of newly polished steel. I touched it. It wasn't cold, like steel, but seemed to transmit no temperature, like plastic, or something else; and its balance was perfect, because my slight touch started it turning, glinting and turning, and for all the time I was staying in the mill that blade was never still.

I hardly had time to notice this before my host, Lith, arrived with an older woman. She carried a pile of burlap sacks over her arms, and was smiling. Lith was all business.

"Your name is Seven," he said.

I was disappointed. "That's not very imaginative."

"It has all the letters of the name you gave us, but we substituted an 'n' for the 't.' We don't like 't,' and when you make a simple substitution the letter substituted goes to the end of the name, making your name 'Seven.' "

"That's just a number."

"It's your name while you're here."

He handed me a list off his clipboard. It was a breakdown of the commodities available at the commissary in exchange for work:

1 pr. Coveralls, men	26 hrs.
1 pr. Coveralls, women	29 hrs.
1 lb. Green Tea	07 hrs.
1 red bandanna	01 hr.
1 spoon cocaine.	31 hrs.
1 lemon	0½ hr.
1 lid uncut Columbian	08 hrs.
1 pr. Men's Workshoes	47 hrs.
1 blotter acid	76 hrs.

"You have two days a week to get high, any days you choose. The rest of the week you work. If you want to save your high days, as many of us do, you can work six days a week and do the forty-eight day trip at the end of the year. We have a separate retreat for that. And I don't mean to say that you have to use drugs."

While he was laying this all out for me the woman spread the burlap sacks in one corner for a makeshift bed. She sat down on it. She looked nearly fifty, but had a lovely, slim body noticeable under her shift.

"You might decide by morning what kind of work you'd like to do around here," said Lith, as he left.

"What's your name?" I asked the woman.

"Marie," she said, standing up and laying both her arms on my shoulders. Her smile was nice.

"What was your name before you came here?"

"Marie. My name was always Marie."

"Didn't you have to change your name?"

"That's Lith's trip. It's a power number he does. He's always doing that."

"You mean I didn't have to change my name. My name can still . . ."

She put her fingers over my mouth. "Seven. Seven is a nice name. Don't worry."

We turned once in the closing darkness. For the first time since I received my parcel of wrists I feel an emotion stronger than my curiosity. It's frightening. I know it won't last.

"It's so weird, you staying here. I mean like no one else has ever stayed in this building. I mean, you know, I wanted to make it with you the first minute I saw you, but I don't think I can get it on with anyone in this building. No way." She releases me and backs off, shaking her head. Her voice is young and sweet and troubled as a trippy teen-ager's. It is strange to watch this lovely white-haired woman, carrying her years so well, but spouting an anomalous youthful jargon. A bell rings in the yard, like a Chinese gong.

"Food time," she says. I follow her to the mess hall.

When I got back to my building the blade was still turning, and though it was dark it still glinted, reflecting light from some invisible source. I moved my bed of burlap sacks into the semicircle of reflected light. When I lay down the turning light flowed over my face like a cool fabric. I slept well in the light, as if I were back under the streetlamp outside my New York bedroom window.

The work I was going to do at the commune had already chosen itself. As soon as I woke up I began to check out the machinery. It was stiff. It wanted a good dousing in penetrating oil to get it turning. The belts were brittle and needed to be soaked in neat's-foot oil. I had to rehabilitate an old generator to power the operation. Other people at the commune, once they saw what I was up to, pitched in. They realized the sawmill was a possible source of income, if they could cut selectively and sell the abundant hardwood in their forest. I worked continuously, finding in myself a capacity for hard labor I had never felt before, and an aptitude, even inventiveness in dealing with this machinery that seemed to be so clear, continuous, and elegant a process of cause and effect — this shaft turns that cog drives this belt — that it was relaxing to contemplate, and exhilarating to

work on. The result would be (I relished the prospect) that I would
have the privilege of watching that wonderful blade, that peculiarly
elegant presence that reflected, or perhaps even generated, the light
over my sleep; I would have the privilege of being the witness to its
first cut.

I haven't felt so good ever in my life, eating fresh soy beans and
squash and collards and okra, feasting on whole grains, taking milk
and butter from the goats kept here. If my life were mine to choose
I certainly would choose to live this way. Marie has gotten over her
phobia about staying in the mill now that it seems populated, although she still refuses to sleep with me under the light of the blade.
When she arrives we move the burlap into a corner and make love
with a tenderness I've never known before, and a mutual appreciation
that makes every touch, every stroke exquisite. If she stays away, or
if she leaves when it's still dark, I move my burlap back near the saw
blade that has become my obsession now that I live on this commune.

I don't know how long it took me to get the mill into working
condition, but I got it done. In the evening at dinner I announced the
completion of my work and everyone at the commune cheered. Lith
rose, and in a quite old-fashioned way, proposed a toast to me. He
raised his glass of carrot juice and carried on about how Seven came,
and Seven worked, and Seven was now one of them. They all clicked
glasses. Someone proposed they allow me a bonus of twenty-five
hours credit at the commissary. I accepted. I traded that windfall for
a pair of leather suspenders, made in the commune, tooled with a
pattern of daisies and swastikas, which I wear even to this day.

The mill was to be launched on the following afternoon according
to a ritual of their own devising, which Marie described to me as a
Cherokee Thanksgiving ritual modified by Shaker austerity. She
thought I would appreciate it. Part of the austerity, she explained,
was that she abstain from making love with me the night before the
inaugural. I lie on my mat alone in the saw-light and stare at the
blade. How tempting it is to start the works and make the first cut
myself. This is not my commune, I think, but it is my mill, after all.

I stand up and go outside. The moon is full behind a nappy
blanket of bright little clouds. I heft a piece of the black walnut tree
I cut that afternoon out of the woods. A certain energy seems to fill
me. To hell with it, I'll do it. I pile a lot of sacks around the generator to muffle the sound and start it up. No one seems to stir. I enter
the mill and lay the piece of walnut on the saw-table. The wood is

cylindrical, about three feet long, and two feet in diameter. I don't know why, but I anticipate that the first cut from my saw will be something special. I pull the lever and engage the gears. All the wheels in the room start to turn. I throw another lever and without a hum the saw blade picks up momentum. I feed the small log into it by hand. There is no sound as the blade easily rips the wood. It is like drawing a line across a sheet of paper, as if the blade were inking the separation of the wood into halves. They fall apart. I shut off the blade and generator. The two halves are perfect, shining as if they had been minutely sanded. They look like two surfaces of polished stone. There is no sawdust left on the table.

I put my bed back in Marie's corner and left the mill. I expect the commune has made good use of it since my departure. I climbed into the truck that went early every morning to Hohenwald and fell asleep, hiding under some mats. By seven I was in Hohenwald, and by three that afternoon I arrived at the Nashville station.

"You're the fellow from Irondale," said Vincent D'Ambrogio. I was learning the luxury of being shaved by a barber familiar with your face.

"Yep, I'm from Irondale."

I bought the yellow Mustang for seventy-five dollars. It was in pretty good running condition; at least, good enough to get me from Nashville to Iron City, where I was headed next, and back again if it was necessary. To get to Iron City you take Route 431 out of Nashville to Franklin, where you get Route 31. Take Route 31 to Columbia until Route 43, which you take to St. Joseph, and from St. Joseph you take an unmarked dirt road to Iron City. That there had been forty-three wrists in the box I received in the morning's mail, and that I was to take Route 43 to get to Iron City, seemed to me no mere coincidence. I was sure I was on the right track.

There's not much happening in Iron City, Tennessee, but it has got a Post Office. It's the small, Deep South town I always imagined I would get to some day. It's on the Alabama border, equidistant from Lawrenceburg, Tennessee, and Florence, Alabama. I felt, when I got out of my Mustang, that I had better not move too fast and call attention to myself from these people who moved so slow they seemed submerged; they lifted their heads and slowly raised their eyelids to register my presence. Black people, white people, they all looked like Southerners to me. They almost smiled. They weren't used to strangers. I could feel my heart beating so quickly and erratically it seemed to rattle in my chest. I sat down at a little lunch counter called Louise for breakfast, and she served me grits and golden eggs and the thickest, sweetest bacon I have ever tasted.

It took me a while to get up the nerve to go to the Post Office across the street. A few people sat around over there, saying some words, among the four squat Doric columns that fronted the building. I had no sane purpose for being in Iron City, Tennessee, especially since the wrinkled piece of wrapping paper I had carried in my pocket from New York City was post marked without a smudge, from Irondale, Tennessee.

There was just one wicket in the Post Office behind which no one seemed present in the vast, empty space used for the receiving, sorting, and holding of mail. It's clear that not much mail comes through Iron City, Tennessee, an observation that makes me hopeful the postmaster will remember such a parcel of wrists as I received in the morning's mail, if indeed it was sent from this place. I saw no one anywhere behind the wicket. For several minutes I read the Wanted posters tacked to the dark brown wood paneling. America is full of fugitives it seems to me. No one appears. I step outside. Several people sit on the porch of the Post Office. "Is there anybody working in the Post Office?" I inquire. Everyone turns to look at someone I take at first to be a young man, but who I realize after a moment is a young woman, very attractive, although dressed to disguise her beauty in a pale beige uniform like a state trooper's without badges, her long black hair coiled in a tight braid against the back of her head.

"I'm the postal clerk," she says. Several other people, a young boy, a smoky old man, an old woman in a long cotton smock, all get up to leave, as if my presence is too much for them to handle.

"I need some stamps," I say.

She smiles. It's the first real smile I've noticed since I pulled into Iron City. "I think we've got some left," she says. "I'll see you inside." I enter and watch through the wicket. She gets in through the back door. She seems more handsome every moment, erect, yet mobile and graceful. She unlocks her stamp drawer and thumbs through the folder more like a collector than a postal clerk. She grins at me.

"We have several 1½¢ stamps, three 17¢, and one 90¢. There'll be a new shipment next week. They seem to disappear as soon as we get them."

I laid my piece of wrapping paper on the counter in front of her eyes. "Do you know this person?" I asked.

She looked at my face, taking in my short hair and my blue eyes. I noticed something in her dark eyes beyond Irondale, Tennessee.

"Are you a detective?"

"Yes," I replied.

She examined both sides of the paper and handed it back to me.

"This is postmarked Irondale, Tennessee."

"There is no Irondale, Tennessee," I said.

"O. I didn't know that," she said, scrutinizing the paper again. "I thought that if there was a postmark there always was a place."

"Not in this case," I said. "But if somebody by the name of C. Routs lives in this town I would like to speak to him."

"So would I," she said, coyly. "But I never heard of such a name, and I know all the names. Can you tell me what was in the parcel you received?"

I looked away from her, down at the brass counter. "Forty-three human wrists," I said, almost gagging on the words.

When I look up she is smiling at me as if she really likes me. "Were they gift wrapped?" she asks.

"No. No." I say. "Not at all."

"That seems even more peculiar. You'd think if someone sent them, went to all that trouble, he'd want to wrap them nicely." She locks up her stamp drawer. Everything suddenly seems easier to me; if not clearer, at least less complicated. "Do you have a car?" she asks. I say that I have a yellow Mustang.

"Good," she says. "I'm closing the Post Office for the rest of the day, and I need a ride home."

A crowd had gathered around my yellow Mustang while I was in the Post Office. I made my way through them and got to the car door. "Wouldn't you know it was a Yankee," said a man in the crowd. Then I saw what had made the crowd gather. A large bird, a buzzard, somehow had got into the car and was perched on the driver's seat. I had locked the car up before breakfast at Louise and had no idea how the bird could get in.

"How do it feel ridin' shotgun to a buzzard?" asked someone under a straw hat. I opened the door and the buzzard lurched once, tumbled out of the car, and then with laborious grace lifted itself above the crowd where it circled easily. The crowd dispersed. I thought to myself, "How strange."

I could hardly keep my eyes on the road with the postal clerk beside me. Cynthia was her name. She was from Mobile, Alabama, but had gone to school in the North and had shed some of her accent there. As we rode into the bronze shade of tobacco country she began to let down her braid and slowly comb it out. Her hair was very long and very black, and I kept losing my eyes in it. Only her hand, occasionally touching mine on the wheel, reminded me that I was driving.

"This is home," she says. Just as I pull into her red-dirt driveway she wraps around her forehead a brightly beaded headband of exquisite design. I don't know what to expect next. I don't expect anything. The day composes itself minute by minute.

Cynthia lives in a large, circular house of yurtlike construction set in off the road among some loblolly pines. The sharecropper land around their place is in sorghum and cotton. A bearded man steps out of the front door and comes toward us. I am disappointed. He takes my hand. "It's good to see you, man. It's really good to see somebody." He throws an arm around my shoulder and leads me into the house he had built himself. "I tell you, sometimes I'm so strung out here. It's lonely, man. Nobody. I'm a city boy, and this is a strange trip for me, though I love it somehow, sometimes; but sometimes I think I've got to get away."

I won't describe the elaborate ornaments they have made for their circular home. They were both accomplished craftsmen. While Cynthia was changing her clothes her boyfriend, named Kevin, told me their history. He and Cynthia had come as Vista volunteers, had been dismissed because of budget cuts, and decided to stay anyway, bought a little piece of land, and because of her father's political pull Cynthia had landed the postal clerk's job, a real plum in Lawrence County. It all made me yawn. For so long I had been indulging myself in my own luxuriously inexplicable activity, that the utter mundanity of this beautiful couple's history made me want to sleep. When Cynthia appeared again in jeans and a Pakistani blouse I realized I preferred her in her trooper's uniform, so ephemerally possible underneath. In this youth culture outfit she was just another pretty girl.

"Let's go," she said.

"Where are we going?"

"We've got some distance to travel," said Kevin. "There's something you need to see."

"What is it?"

"You'll see it," said Cynthia.

I smiled and slapped my toe on the gas. That was an exchange of information on a level I found pleasurable. We traveled East for miles, into more mountainous country. Kevin kept a Jew's harp in his mouth which he plucked at random on the way, while Cynthia leaned against him and hummed. It was late afternoon. The shadows were deep in the foothills. "I think it's just over the next hill," Kevin kept saying. I took his word for it and drove. It wasn't over the next hill, or the next one. What we finally came on looked to me at first like a gravel pit for the highway department. Except there was a difference. People were swarming throughout the excavation, among the idle bulldozers and graders. They were scrounging in the rubble. They were ripping at the perimeter of turf. Hundreds of them. An old woman, emaciated Appalachian lady in a dress of patches, rushed by us, cackling. She carried what looked like a bone of some sort, and a lame old man followed her shouting weakly for her to let him see what she had. The place was full of poor mountain people come down here as if to perform a ritual of disorder in this excavation.

"It's a Cherokee burial ground," said Kevin. "They just came here one day and bulldozed it up. This is on the trail of tears, man. Hundreds of Cherokee starved here, man. Died."

"I'm part Seminole," said Cynthia.

"It's horrible. They just came here and opened it up with bulldozers. It's been full of these people for weeks." A young man ran around in a circle in front of us brandishing what looked like a piece of human jaw. He was really happy.

"I haven't slept," said Kevin. "Since they excavated this place. I don't know what's happening, but we've got to get away from here."

"I'm part Cherokee," said Cynthia.

I wandered away from Kevin and Cynthia, in among the people grubbing for relics. Things weren't as chaotic as they had first seemed.

Territories in the pit seemed to be tacitly assumed by family groups. That organization made the activity seem not quite so horrible. Everyone: children, adults, old people, were working furiously at unearthing whatever was there. The mountain air was full up with delirious vibrations, like the screeching of brakes. Their faces were full of it, the demonic glee of Americans unspeakably poor suddenly getting for free something that might be valuable, that they insisted on making valuable with their own intensity. They rushed around waving skulls and legbones, showing fistfuls of arrowheads and pottery shards. One family had planted a post; and on it they were carefully reconstructing with bailing wire the complete skeleton of a Cherokee youth. They were such a poor family, such a flea-bitten lot of enthusiastic kids, and they lavished on their primitive archeological project so much attention and love that I surprised myself by starting to weep. How long it has been since I last wept. I watched them carefully trying to fit bones into place, their own arms so thin, scarcely more than some bones to begin with.

I had enough. It is almost dark. People are leaving in old pickups and junk cars and tractors with carts. I look for my car. It's gone. Kevin and Cynthia have escaped. I'm alone. It doesn't get me mad. It's not so bad that they took the yellow Mustang. I was through with it, and it was through with me; but my sheepskin coat is in the car, and now I'm cold. It's dark. I'll have to stick it out for a whole night in these mountains, by this excavated Indian boneyard. I climb to the woods above the hole and scrape up a pile of leaves to crawl into for warmth, my boy scout notion of survival in the wilderness. There is no way I can get to sleep in this place. Down there the people are digging through the night. They are orange with huge, swaying shadows in the light of fires they have lit to illuminate their work. Some play harmonicas and banjoes and sing spirituals. Their music is subtle, lustrous, like something valuable. I consider prayer for myself. What can prayer mean as I remember speaking it as a child, spoken by my voice in this location, in the fix I am in, among the homeless spirits of the Cherokee that wander abroad this evening?

I got on the road and hitched back to New York in the morning. My long evening awake had made me do a lot of thinking. The possibility that most nagged me was that I had been wrong about the wrists. Perhaps I had mistakenly perceived wrists, and there had been something else entirely in the package: some flexible plastic cable or some kind of sausage. It was important that I get back to my apartment and dig one up; after all, forty-three is an odd number.

The New York I returned to was not the New York I had left. There was such an hysteria in the air, such broad currents of ill will inundating the faces of people in the streets that I hardly recognized the place where I had spent the most exciting years of my development as a human being. As soon as I opened the door to my apartment the telephone rang. That was a sound I hadn't heard for a while.

"Steve. I'm so glad you're home. This is Nikki. God, my voice must really sound different. I need to talk to you. Michael's in the hospital."

"Get him out of there."

"He was stabbed. We were mugged."

I glanced into the other room where I had left my forty-three potted wrists. Something had happened in there while I was gone. I couldn't say a word into the telephone. I tried to get my coat off. Something green was happening in the other room.

"Are you still there?"

"Yes." The word peeled off the top of my palate.

"I need to speak to you. I need to see you."

I was peering into the other room. I began to shake because I suddenly had the premonition that of all the strange changes that had come down since I received my parcel of wrists, the most shattering were just beginning to develop.

"Are you there?"

"I'm there." I'd forgotten I was holding the telephone.

"Listen. I have to come over. Will that be okay?"

"Come over," I said. "It's okay." I hung up. Without taking my eyes off the other room I put my coat away. There was certainly a presence in there. I reached around the doorway and switched on the light, and without entering at first I scrutinized the contents. What I saw filled me suddenly with a feeling I can only call joy in our language, but it was a terrifying joy, a feeling that seemed balanced in me on the most delicately equilibrated pinnacles, and my premonition was that if I refused to nurture this feeling I would totter off into an abysmal silence. Happiness settled from nowhere on my chest, and rushed out as pure laughter from my parted lips. In each of the forty-three pots something had sprouted. My room was full of greenery.

They were tiny, monocotyledonous plants that came up on slender stems, each so far producing a single large leaf with a wavy margin. Each of the pots had produced one of these graceful plants, and there was no way I could bring myself to disturb any of them at the roots. I couldn't dig one up now. I touched the soil. It was very dry. My first responsibility would be to water them. I needed some grow-lights, some fishmeal fertilizer. Larger pots for transplanting.

I open the door to leave for the plant store and find myself face to face with two women. "You have a sixth sense," says Nikki.

"Why are you wearing your overcoat and carrying that teapot?" asks the other woman.

"I brought Linda. I hope it's okay," says Nikki. "I'm afraid to go out in the street by myself just now."

It feels as if I never left the city. Linda is the woman with whom I was having a rather desultory affair before the arrival of my wrists. She is smart and pretty, a promising young editor at a small, prestigious publishing house, one of the bright, young, independent women of our time; but when we are alone together each sucks the other into such emptiness, such a vast, unremitting indifference to one another, each of us pledged to his and her own vague ambitions, that our relationship is an excruciating game that we both find to be evil, and therefore addicting. We are seen together. We are presumed to be together. Indeed we are still attracted to each other like some barely luminous plankton in the great, tidal, disjunctive movement of life in New York City. Enough of that.

"Last night it was raining, you know. We were walking down Broadway without an umbrella, just getting wet. It was nice. Michael noticed two guys with an umbrella fall in step behind us as we turned down 78th Street. I could feel Michael's arm get tense. I turned around and saw them. They were two black guys. Michael knew what was coming. He picked up the pace and crossed the street, and we started back for Broadway where there would be some people. It was too late. They backed us against the wall. One held the umbrella and a gun. The other had a straight razor that he kept at Michael's face as he took his wallet. They were smiling. They didn't say anything. I became hysterical. 'Don't hurt him. He's a great writer. He's your friend. Rape me. Don't hurt him.' I spouted all sorts of self-destructive nonsense."

"That's your negative sexism. It's pitiful," says Linda.

"Whatever it was it didn't work. The guy with the umbrella

thanked me for the invitation. He was young and really fine looking. I was actually weirdly attracted to him. Maybe I really thought I could win him with love. I don't know. Anyway, the guy with the razor slashed Michael's face twice, in an X right across one eye, then he ripped his stomach. I'm sure they would have done something to me next, but a patrol car turned the corner, and I screamed, and the dome light and siren went on, and the two muggers sprinted, and now Michael is in the hospital. He's critical."

While Nikki is telling her story I prepare some tea on my hotplate. I always take a lot of care with tea. I like it. This time it is Mormon tea, or squaw tea, made from twigs of the creosote bush, mixed with a touch of damiana, a Mexican herb, for its aroma. You drop that tea into the boiling water, then shut off the heat. Nikki stands up as the brew is steeping and starts to cry. She embraces me. A shudder travels up her spine, connecting with me at the navel and loosening my knees. "I'm sorry. I'm sorry. I'm sorry," she says. I say something perfunctory. She sits down. I pour the tea. Linda sips and watches both of us. I am trembling as Nikki is trembling.

"I've never been mugged. Almost all my friends have," says Linda. "It's just never happened to me. Must be my vibes."

I've neglected what is going on in the other room. I glance momentarily at the bedroom door, and then at Linda. She smiles slightly and lowers her eyelids. She thinks what I mean is that I want her to stay the night. I don't know how to refute that assumption. Nikki sees our exchange and understands the same thing as Linda. She sighs.

"I'll take a cab home. I guess all I wanted was to see a man I knew. I'll be all right."

"I think I can visit Michael tomorrow." I say.

"It would be good to go together. I'd appreciate it," says Nikki. I take her hand as we're flagging a cab. The hand is so cold it's almost painful to hold it.

When I got back to my apartment Linda had opened the door to my bedroom, and was standing just inside, surveying my growing patriarchy.

"Steve," she said, turning to me. "I didn't know you had such a green thumb."

I was amazed. What a few moments before had been nothing more than a few limber seedlings were now, all of them, healthy plants, almost two feet high, splendidly leafed out, and they had grown that fast without fertilizer or grow-light, just a little New York City water. "It's not that so much," I said. "They just grow."

"How did you get them?"

"They came in the mail." I almost told her about the wrists, but decided it would take too much energy to explain, and she would think I was putting her on in some male way, or that I was going totally nuts, as she had always anticipated.

"Amazing," she said. "I never get anything in the mail." She stared at me. "I like you without the beard. The hair could be longer for my taste, though."

We turned off the light, undressed, and immediately started to make love. It was horrible. So little did we love each other that we couldn't tolerate any mischief, any foreplay, any giggling conversation. We went at each other and satisfied our needs. We had each other, and stopped. Linda fell asleep under the blankets. I lay awake on top of them in the light of the mercury vapor lamp on my corner, casting pale shadows from the leaves of my garden across my body. The shadows felt warm. I didn't dare sleep. Two children's stories kept playing in my head: Jack and the Beanstalk and Pandora's Box. They were the potential nightmares that kept me awake.

Linda left before breakfast that morning, and I rushed out to buy growlights , fertilizer, and the larger pots, which I already needed. I also got a botanical key, and a book by Thalassa Cruso on potted plants. I took almost all my money, but there was no way I could scrimp on this new responsibility. Was it a hobby? Was it an avocation? Was it my new path? The plants ahd begun to so appropriate my energy and integrate my time with their welfare that my decision had to be that this was now my life. I should have hated the idea, but I didn't. I knew that I would have to get a job, and keep it, no screwing around any more if my plants were to survive. What a novel and exhausting cause has arisen to absorb me. What a fool I am.

There's very little more to tell about it. I got a job writing ad copy, and it brings in enough. From that evening on I allowed no visitors to my apartment. The plants have expanded their territory from my bedroom to the living room and kitchen. They have grown to be quite the little trees. I haven't yet been able to identify them. When they were small I thought they might have been some sweet

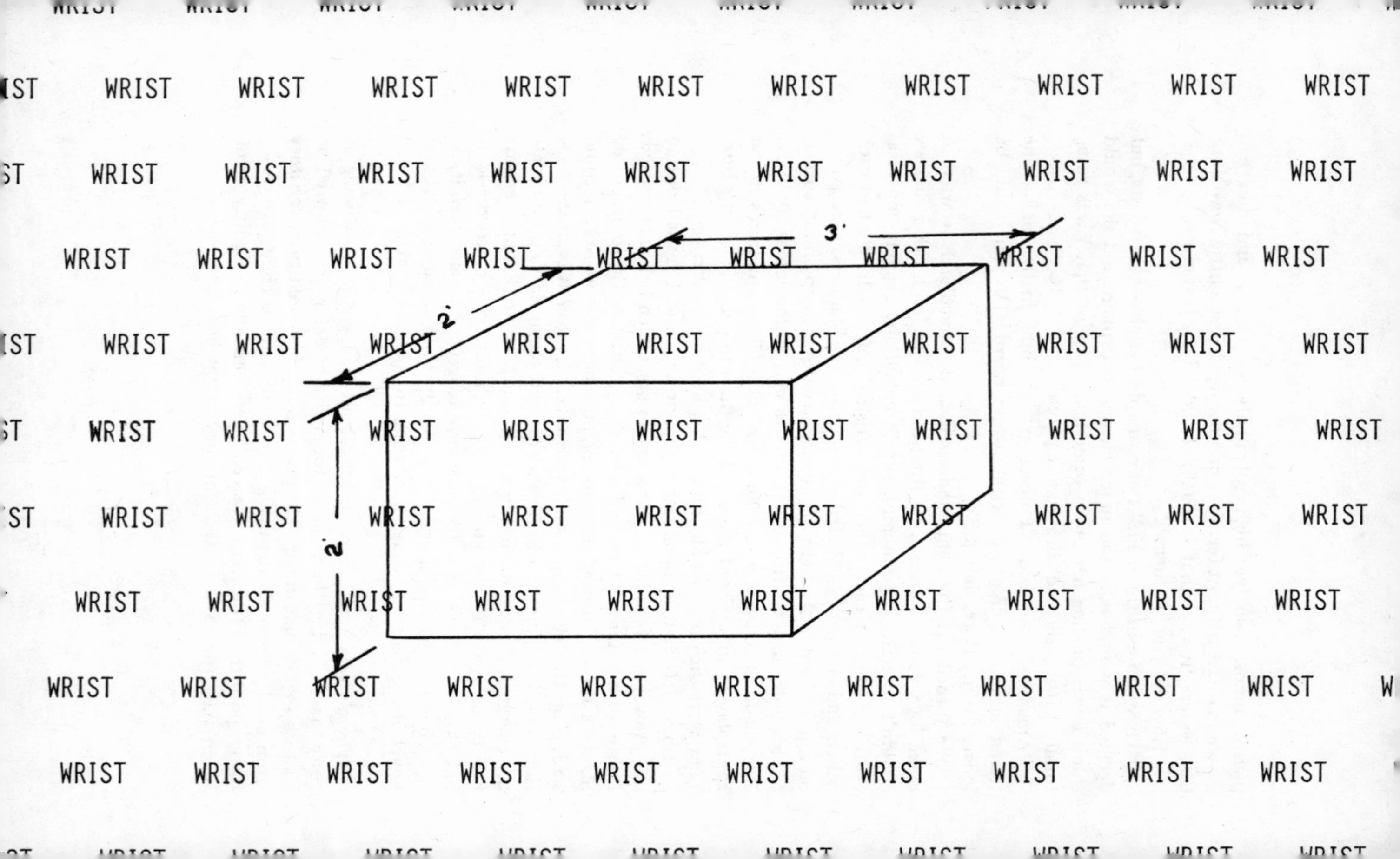

viburnum or nannyberries (*Viburnum lentago Linnaeus*), but I learned that except for greenbriers most woody plants are dichotyle-
donous. As the plants grew the new leaves became thicker and deeper green, as if they might be related to the lemon or some other
citrus. I thought, when blossoms began to appear, that I would finally
have the decisive clue to the identity of my plants, and perhaps to
the mystery of my parcel of wrists, wrists that since I received them
in the morning mail have never been off my mind, lying there like
the skies above me full of little clouds.

Not so. The blossoms were quite unusual. They were odorless.
Although the forty-three plants were superficially identical, they each
put out a different blossom, and each of the blossoms on the same
plant differed one from the other in some small particular of shape
or size or behavior; I could describe them forever. Some grew in
clusters, some singly, some drooped, some erect. One of the flowers
was made of insects, tiny gray-golden flies clustered around a stem
like lupine or larkspur, that scattered when you got close, the flower
seeming to disappear in a scintillation of these little flies, then re-
appearing when you withdrew. One that looked like Indian paint-
brush would curl itself around your finger if you tried to touch it.
Another, like a small peony, would lean towards you as you got
close, and seem to pucker up as if it had the urge to give you a kiss.
Each flower was a different color; not just a shade, but a distinct
color. My mind is now full of ten thousand colors, colors that are
nowhere visible, that even Fra Angelico could never have touched to
canvas.

That they were invariably odorless made me uneasy, because
there's always a certain aloofness about a flower without a smell, as
if there is something they want to hold back from the world of men.

As demanding as the plants were while they grew and flowered,
they complicated my life even further when they began to bear fruit.
I had begun to like the way things were shaping up for me. Granted,
my territory in the apartment I share with my forest has been reduced to a corner near the bathroom, where I have my bed, my
telephone, and my hot plate; but everything is very compact, and I
like it. I come home, spend a few hours watering and observing the
brood, and go to sleep. I have come to like the noise the plants make
at night, as if they are inventing a wind for themselves, but now the
fruit begins to appear and the relative simplicity of my life is changing.

I got home late after visiting Michael in the hospital, and having dinner with Nikki. Michael not only lost the sight in one eye but also lost the ability to control the movement of the other. Nikki was very upset, and blamed as much as she could on me. She mentioned my aloofness. I'm not compassionate enough. She told me I don't give enough time to my friends. She mentioned a group that she and Linda go to that she thought I ought to join. They all get together, men and women, and rap about their problems, getting it all out in the open; and then they have their problems out there in the open, ready to share. I thas been a long time since I thought of myself as having problems, although I do recognize as problematical my time-consuming charter of responsibilities. Nonetheless when I got home I was quite upset. There is nothing, not even death, so unnerving as a close friend suddenly blinded.

I have difficulty falling asleep; but just as I have about broken through all the fine charged wires of consciousness, and am nearly away, I hear a loud thunk, as of a large book dropping on a table, and my eyes snap open. It was one of those noises that you can't locate in space. I thought it came from out there, but its reverberations remain confined to my skull. I lie there looking out, expecting the noise to repeat. It doesn't, but I'm awake for the duration. I turn the lights off and wander into my forest. At first I don't notice anything has changed, except the unusual quiet. Then I notice that all the petals have fallen, all at once, not a hint of flowers on the trees; and then, as if my eyes have suddenly adjusted to the peculiar sight I am obliged to witness, I notice the kind of fruit my parcel of trees has begun to bear. I work my way toward a slight whisper in the corner. There, one of the trees has produced, on slender, flexible stems, like an abundance of cherries, a crop of human lips. They are all moving, cleverly using the leaves nearest to themselves for tongues. As I get closer to them I hear them saying, "Find me some teeth. Get me some teeth."

Perhaps I am dreaming. It's the kind of dream I would have, the way my life has been going. Two things happen to assure me I'm not. I feel a sudden blow on my rump from the rear, and the telephone rings. I turn to see that I have been kicked by a tree whose limbs are weighed down with a crop of human legs, like bunches of bananas. It seems like such a ridiculously slapstick apparition that I break out laughing, and I am still laughing as I pick up the telephone.

"Do you always wake up laughing?" Linda asks.

"I've been awake," I say.

"I always think I'm the only one who isn't able to sleep," she says, and she goes on talking as I survey my forest of parts. There is something else on each of the forty-three trees: noses, armpits, navels, knees, vaginas and penises, pelvises. The sight is terrifying and exhilarating.

I agreed to meet Linda for dinner in the evening. She hung up, and I stared into my woods still holding the receiver. Sleep came on me suddenly there in the wooden chair, my eyes open.

Michael seems somewhat unnerved to have me pop in on him at the hospital on the next day, but I have no choice. I have the means to help him, and if a friend has those means he should use them, whatever the sacrifice.

"Of course I want to see. Are you crazy? I still like to see."

He isn't prepared for me. He hasn't been properly tranquilized. I can feel hysteria near the surface of his skin. There is a bandage over the socket of the eye he has lost, and over the wandering eye is a black patch to help him avoid the confusion of seeing. He lifts the patch and tries to look at me. I can't be but a blur, some streaks of color in the random, rapid motion of his vision. The eyeball jerks around out of control in his skull. I put my hand on his forearm and feel the sobs coming from his belly.

"I'm sorry," I say.

"It's not your fault," he says. "I'll get used to it."

I feel the time is right. "I think I've got something to help you." I reach into the bag in my pocket and pull out one of the eyes I just picked fresh this morning. Only the brown eyes have ripened so far but I feel it should still be at least a temporary consolation, even though Michael's eyes are blue. He seems calm for the moment. I hold the eye with the tips of my fingers over his own flailing eye and try to follow the movement so he can see, at least for the moment, what I have brought him.

At this point something very unexpected happens. At first I don't know it's happening, but then I realize that my arm is moving, without my intending it; indeed, if I wanted to I couldn't do it. The arm is moving in perfect synchronization with what I imagine to be the random motion of Michael's injured eye. I am following it. It isn't difficult. I can feel in my fingertips the eye I have brought making minute adjustments of angle and focus. Then I suddenly perceive, or begin to understand that I am beginning to see through the palm of my hand. I close my eyes. At first I see only the surface of Michael's blue eye, in its absolute stillness; and then I begin to see through his eye, or behind his eye, the image clearing through my palm. What I see is a huge tree, like a giant lush maple, with a bifurcated trunk. One half of the tree is full of squirrels, chasing each other in circles; on the other half a great black-and-white hawk preens its feathers and sharpens its beak against the limb it is gripping. Behind the tree a sun, distended, ovoid, at the horizon, is either rising or setting. I don't have time to see if it's going up or down because someone has grabbed my arm and has made me drop the eye. All this time, Michael has been screaming. Two orderlies pull me back from the bed. I don't resist. I feel sorry for Michael.

"Jesus, Maria, look what he's got," says one of the orderlies, as the bag falls from my pocket and my eyes all roll across the floor. One of the orderlies lets go of me to scoop up the eyes, and in a moment of self-preservation I break the grip of the other orderly and get out of there, escaping through the emergency exit. I realize that now life is going to be very hard for Michael, unless he figures out how to help himself, and despite the fact that I have suffered no physical injury from now on life will be almost impossible for me, and there is no way I can help it.

Linda and I met that evening at a Japanese restaurant on West 56th Street. At first we had little to say to each other. We didn't want to talk about Michael or Nikki because we both already knew too much. She was too considerate to burden me with publishing gossip, and I didn't have much I wanted to tell her from my own life. We ate iced bean curd, and sushi, and pickled radish. It was a refreshing meal, and as a result we both were very relaxed. I sighed and she sighed.

"Steve," she said "I wish I knew where our relationship was going."

I smiled and watched her face very carefully. She leaned forward and took both my hands, which I had carelessly left on the table. "I do love you," she said.

I have always been obsessed with watching Linda's mouth. It is her most expressive feature. It tends, in fact, to telegraph her feelings, to demonstrate them on such a level of exaggeration, so much sadness weighing down the lips, so much passion in their pucker, that when I was in a more intimate position not of watching her, but of being a subject of love, I would find myself hurtling off on long blind journeys of guilt or horniness just from noticing her mouth. That evening her lips seemed to flash a curious mixed semaphor of love, pain, despair, indifference, defensiveness, abandon: every nuance. I slipped one of my hands out of hers, and took from my inside jacket pocket a large billfold and picked from it one of the lovelier sets of lips I had gleaned from my tree. I leaned forward and attached them to her mouth. They made a world of difference.

"What do you call that?" she said, puckering up and working her mouth around, finally peeling the new lips off and dropping them into her hand. The lips immediately flipped over and kissed her on the palm. "What is all this you've got here?" she giggled. I already had another set out and was trying it on her. She wiped that one off and then dumped my cache of lips out of my billfold onto the table. They squirmed around there, kissing each other, and kissing her hand. She drew back, amused and horrified at the same time. "What are these things?"

I was too absorbed in the problem I saw in front of me to answer. I pulled a few chins out of another pocket. There is such a variety of chins. I tried to line a dimpled one up on Linda's face, but when she saw it she covered that face as if horrified. It was unfortunate. I pulled the noses and ears on her. I had made a careful selection. "You're crazed. I always knew it would happen to you. You're absolutely insane." When she saw I was insisting on what I was doing she stood up at the table. "Steve, I'm going to leave before I start screaming and embarrass us both." She threw on her shawl and rushed out the door. I looked around the restaurant and the few people who had been staring our way went back to manipulating their chopsticks. The waitress, an older Japanese woman in traditional dress, who looked perpetually worried, started to clear the table. I gathered my produce back into my pockets, paid my bill, and went into the streets. Though I understood Linda's point of view I was disappointed. I had been hoping I could depend on a few old friends.

Old friends dropped away. Nothing I could do about it. My commitment wasn't the result of any decision I had made and for that reason was all the more binding. I was doomed from then on to make a kind of pest out of myself. Perhaps you have met me at one time or another in the streets, haunting strangers, insisting on the replacements from the pack of goods I carry on my back. You must know who I am.

Occasionally I do meet someone who knows who I am, who has even come looking for me. It's gratifying and disconcerting. I remember a girl by the name of Susan Kentucky. She met me on the street, said she'd come all the way from Atlanta, Georgia, just to find me. She took me to lunch, not even ashamed to sit with me among all the flashy people at the Buffalo Roadhouse. She had a hamburger, I had a spinach salad. It was tasty. And it wasn't like being with Linda that time. She said, "You do have style, Steve. I really like your style." It was flattery, and I appreciated that in itself. I was far beyond the inclination to make the so-called "next move," but some move was possible because flattery is often more liberating than the truth. I did begin to lay out my goods for her, never imagining that someone who had looks as perfect as Susan Kentucky's would use any of it. She took a forehead, complete with temples, a couple of cheeks with variable dimples, one of my most powerful brows, and I don't know what else. I was a success. She offered to pay for it all. How could I let her pay for anything? I was in love with Susan Kentucky, as I am secretly in love with everyone else.

I don't imagine I'll ever see her again. There's no reason for her to look for me any more, and if she has applied my parts to her features I'll never be able to recognize her. That's one of the hazards of my occupation, and one of the paradoxes not entirely taken into account by those who imagine mine to be a "power trip." Who is it? Who really exercises the control. That's an important question.

I sometimes try to put my finger on the one problem that caused this life that I have, to all intents and purposes, lived, to take the peculiar turn it did at a certain point. I think it's that I never really trusted the United States Post Office. I didn't really believe in it. If I had I would have done what I should have done in the first place when I received my parcel of wrists in the morning mail. Without thinking about it I should have wrapped it up again and shipped it back to C. Routs in Irondale, Tennessee, where it came from. When I consider it from this vantage I realize that could have made all the difference. If I had done that my life might have worked itself out by an entirely other set of priorities.

TEN POEMS

FRANCISCO BRINES

Translated by Louis M. Bourne

TRANSLATOR'S NOTE: The work of Francisco Brines, unlike that of other post-Civil War Spanish poets, deals not so much with man's social as his metaphysical condition. Its starting point is autobiographical, and its implications, tragic. Brines sees life as a series of pleasant interludes in an unswerving course toward death. Though he shares something of his fellow poet Carlos Bousoño's apocalyptic manner (see Bousoño's "Ten Poems" in ND24), his foreshadowing of life's completion is unaccompanied by any transcendental vision. In this respect, he resembles a classical or pagan poet, reared without a god.

Brines was born in Oliva (Valencia) in 1932. He received a degree in law from the University of Salamanca, another in literature from the University of Madrid and, for two years, he was a lecturer in Spanish literature at Oxford University. Brines now lives in Madrid.

His first work, Las brasas *("The Embers," awarded the Premio Adonais), appeared in 1960. This was followed by* El Santo Inocente *("The Innocent Saint," 1965),* Palabras a la oscuridad *("Words to Darkness," 1966), which won the coveted Premio de la Crítica, and* Aún no *("Not Yet," 1971). Brines's collected poems were published*

161

in 1974 under the title Poesia 1960-1971: Ensayo de una despedida
*("Poetry 1960-1971: Dry-run for a Farewell"). Since then, he has
completed another volume,* Insistencia en Luzbel *("Insistence on
Lucifer," 1976).*

Brines's poetry is the result of the struggle between head and heart:
*a lucid intelligence that directs a stoical, pessimistic, yet no less brave
acceptance of life's enslavement to time; and an often hedonistic
desire to experience love and sensuous pleasures. He tempers an epi-
curean yearning with a fatalist's sense of resignation before the follies
of human existence, and with a moral recognition that good poetry
displays a "keenness for knowledge" while it "revives our passion
for life."*

THE ROOM IS IN HALF-LIGHT

The room is in half-light, invaded
By declining sun, red lights that
Change the orchard in the glass, and someone
Who's a mass of shadow is seated.
On the table, the boxes show
Portraits of cities, damp forests
Of ferns, endless beaches, broken
Columns: all the things, like a port,
That thrilled him in boyhood. Before,
He lay on the rug for a long time,
And he conquered adventure. Nothing
Remains of that fervor, and hope
Doesn't live in the present. He slowly
Turns over the pages. This rite
Of dismantling time each day
Gives him a wise look, the custom
Of choosing familiar people
So they might join him. And those
Old lives come back, the youngest
Beloved friends, a certain dead
Woman, and the relatives. He doesn't repeat
The facts as they were; he thinks of them
In a different way, happier, and the landscape

Is filled with a history almost new
(Painful to see, even with deceit,
There's the same ending in dejection).
He remembers a city, of high walls,
Where millions of men live together,
Estranged, alone; he knows
That a look there is like a kiss.
But he loves an island, returns to it
Each night when asleep, and dreams about it
A lot. His tired limbs give up
Their harsh pain when he shuts his eyes
One day he'll set out from the old village
And will sail in a strange boat,
Weightless. Without regret the house
Is left abandoned, the corners now damp
With a coat of moss; the vines, withered;
The books, yellowed. Nobody will ever
Know when he died, the lock will go on
Being covered with a far-off dust.

THE FOREST GROWING DARK

All this beautiful afternoon, of little light,
Fallen over the grey forests of England,
Is time.
        Time that is dying
In my peaceful eyes,
Mixing with time that passes away,
In life, all is
A natural course toward death,
And the free gift that is existence, and breathing,
Breathes and exists toward narrow nothing.

With restful eyes, I watch the forest
Beating with such grace
That this unseen delight that has come into my heart

Seems like a breath of its spirit.
As life in man is completed
So earth's must be as well;
The dim vicinity which is reality now
Will be gloomy distance later,
All will be blackness.

I watch, with these living eyes, the darkness of the forest.
And a deeper delight reaches my heart
When, to the loneliness that chilled me,
Come vanished faces, wavering
Features of some beings
That, with love, look at me, demand company,
Offer me, warm, their ash.
Ringed with growing shadows, I touched my body
And it was barely an ember of heat,
Nearly ash as well.
And then I felt my figure vanishing.

Look how joyfully I tell you
It's beautiful to live.

THE BEGGAR

Strange, on this night, I recall
A vanished image. The beggar
Of my childhood, with hairy face, returns
His harsh look from another world.
He came at noon, and a growl
Of old animal announced him. (All
The house was open, and summer
Was coming in from the sea.) The child
Walked with fear to the door and placed
A coin in his hand. The voice was
Rough, the eyes cold from hate,
And I felt very afraid as I approached,

All pity dispelled. Violently
Death circled round me with its shadow.
Only later, when I saw the grown-ups
Talk indifferently, already back,
Did my heart grow calm. I stayed
Near the window and, facing the sea,
Remembered gloomy stories.

Tonight, so much time gone by,
His terrible and mysterious presence
Keeps me from sleep. I suffered
No harm from that will, and
The man shall have died now, impoverished
As he lived. In those years, many
Other beggars stopped by the houses
Of the village. They all lie below, unavenged.
Oblivion finished them. Vague, broken,
Their shadows spring up; memory stirs
A cold, vast and lonely kingdom.
Powerful, now they give me back
The miserable alms: the pity
That, each day, man needs
To keep on living. And that fear
Which I felt as a child troubles
My life now, its failure: an old man
Looked at me with innocent eyes.

DEATH OF A DOG

for Jacobo Muñoz

Coming into the city
I could see the boys were attacking the dog
And, shouts and howling mixed together, they forced
    him to undo his knot with another's body,
And the mad rush against the wall,
And the terrible stone against the skull,

And many stones more.
And again I see that sudden
Twisting, all his body's dread,
His dizziness when running,
His life spilling from that flexible body,
His life that drained through his open eyes,
Opened wider and wider
For death, with its angry haste, forced him
To desert from within so much substance to be lived,
And only through the eye could it escape;
For there was no light,
For only gloomy shadow arrived.

There among the remains
Of that wall of an unfriendly suburb,
the dog lay spread out;
And now I remember with unexpected anquish
His stiffened head:
His eyes reflect, just like man's
His terror at emptiness.

WALLS OF AREZZO

for Francisco Nieva

Inside that denuded church,
The nave was a shadow, the breath of which
Was a whiff of centuries, and in the depth
We saw light beveling the high wall.
And the human dream ther, with colors
Of the most burning deceit, the ashes
Of a man's desire entombed
In tree, in charger, entourage or angel.
He adds no fantasy or invention:
On the face of man and of earth
He left the required order; and we admire

Not the physical beauty, but the image
Of our quieted flesh. A sum
Of perfection is the human head,
Without fire of glee and without sadness;
Not proud or humbled beneath the arc
Of blue air, so calm his gaze
That it leaves the horses without instinct,
The tree without natural growth.

We are told a history of this world;
The remote excuse of some beings
Like ourselves, but we know
Good and evil here are not passions.
The painted wall shows us the dream
That abolished our dregs: the dying man
And he who loves are the same, kings
And grooms, hills or spears,
Nakedness and fine dress, sun
Or night, the pious and the warrior,
The thirst and the cuirass, the one who guards
And the sleeper in the tent, the lady
And her ladies-in-waiting, the red standard
And the tomb, the young man and the old,
Indifference and pain, God
And man.
            Sometimes when in love,
And making real the old dream
Of a better nature, he wanted
Perfection. Remembering love,
The happiness sustained, his brushes
Preserved the earthly habits and
Gestures, he copied life entire,
And like love, though visible,
There they breathe a thick and lovely air,
Attaining a new order that quiets:
Happy, without freedom, here lives man.

TRUMPET SOLO

for Toni Puchol

When everybody's looks then grew vaguely familiar,
Through pupils clouded over by alcohol,
From that discordant music, from the half-light of that
      smoke, from chaos,
Came an unnoticed silence,
And a single trumpet of fire burned our lives.

Or maybe that music was made of ice:
Lifeless the sounds, so each one of us
Would make them stir, would fill them with spirit.
For each one of the people
The music sang in a different way: with barren joy
In the woman who watched me, with weary sadness
In another's set lips, and, in the lonely boy,
With deep nostalgia for old age;
The music sang in a different way, with no one knowing
How it sounded together, with what intense sorrow.

Nothing in that dark rrom accorded with the truth of man:
The musician's strident emotion was false,
Clumsy the deceit of others.
Truth is humble and it is simple.
Loneliness, when shared with other lonelinesses,
Makes weakness more vivid,
And shoves man then toward heroic regions
With sentiment alone.
Later a weariness falls over the soul
From this useless struggle. One resents
So much false virtue, pretended purity;
And when the trumpet, faltering, dies out in the silence,
Only the most hidden, the most dogged vices stay in sight,
Revealed at last:
The looks show recognition, and there may be pity,
And someone may even feel a lukewarm love.

We see the trumpet
Of fire mute on a table, yellow,
And it's old and scored.

BEGGAR FOR REALITY

You took my hand from yours,
And you've wounded my being.

Now the dogs howl among the pines
And the stars on high harmonize
Light and death.
Dry is the air that dwells in my house,
And memory wanders
Along the roads of dead life.
Frail heat; for where I was happy
A burning shadow lives,
Smoke that I cut through with such pain:
Within the void, a look still
Confers compassion, love, misfortune.
The cave of remembrance is very dark
And it's cold as ice, though it falsifies
The light and heat of home.
This thing we were disintegrates far
From flesh and soul, in the oblivion
Of what has never been. So surely
I know it, so fully I accept it, that it
Hurts no more to think about life's failure.

But, yes, this thirst hurts, this moment
Of spirit and flesh that craves
Happiness of me, though I know well
That, later, it's food for oblivion.
The absence that precedes and the one that follows
Shape our being, but the present
Is known to glow at times.

With a cruel hunger for reality
I howl mutely with the dogs,
I watch the dawn put out the stars,
And I have felt my hand discarded
As though it weren't my own.

HONOR

for Vicente Puchol

Centuries have passed,
And the lie of honor survives glorious,
Like a long fingernail with a mask of silver.
When chained in damp holes
What's noble is secret, love, shameful,
Faith, a soundless rust,
Youth is land destroyed.

We have bought or seduced bodies
In birght-lit avenues, black boats,
Alleys reeking of piss, museums, cathedrals,
Sleepy trains, respectable
Bedrooms and schools without light.
And now I remember, worn-out, the visions
Of some bodies that slip away forever
On the damp clearings,
And the city getting up from the smoke of night,
And the light clawing it coldly.

I have known injury,
The razor sining in,
The arousal of fear,
Living unsatisfied, the hardest negation.
The indifference of some hands
And we walked along looking for the pleasure of the flesh,
The drunken root of fire

And the revulsion there,
Joy springing up unwarranted,
And we have kissed the smile, or its aggravated tremor,
We have felt the misery of being able to give nothing,
      and we were the barren rich,
And have found, delighted, an excuse for practicing pity,
And have known the gloomy life of unknown people,
      have turned it into words,
And have attended, combed and sweet-smelling, the purest
      moment of man's identity.

Now we lift our faces to the night,
And our eyes coldly see
The white light of the hellish moon.

THE WAIT

I
The countryside, dark; far-off, toward the sea,
The lights. And a night bird.

My father is sitting
With the odor of orange between his fingers
And his face silvered. He waits.
And on a long walk
Filled with prayer and tending of jasmine,
My mother is waiting.

Gusts of time
Climb up to the balcony where I watch
Their loneliness, their shadows. In this house
We all wait for somebody to deny us.

II

The countryside, dark; far-off, toward the sea,
The lights. And a night bird.

With his face silvered, and a deep odor
Of orange, a man waits.
And a woman waits, tending
The jasmine. They are two strangers.

I watched from the balcony,
And, on the balcony, there was no one there.

METHODS OF KNOWLEDGE

In the weariness of the night,
Piercing the darkest music,
I recovered behind my blind eyes
The frail evidence of a far-off scene.

The sea smelled, and dawn was thief
Of the skies; the lights of the house
Turned ghostly.
The diners were youths, and, satiated
And without thirst, in the wreck of the banquet,
They sought drunkenness
And the painted procession of joy. Wine
Overflowed the cups, turned
The warm skin pink, reddened the floor.
Their hearts, in generous love, unleashed
The flesh, the word, in the fierce light,
And they didn't mind later not to remember.
Some misdirected dagger sought a heart.

I raised my cup as well, the lightest one,
Filled to the brim with ashes:

Bones of falcon and crossbowman united,
And there I drank, without thirst, two dead experiences,
My heart grew calm, and an innocent child
Covered my head with a madman's cap.

I fixed my lucid eyes
On him who knew how to choose with the surest skill:
That youth who, in a corner, turning his back on all,
Carried a clay cup with poison
To his fresh lips.
                    And, toasting nothingness,
He hurried off into the shadows.

SEVEN POEMS

GUSTAF SOBIN

HELIX

The mist burns
to a bronze whisper.

Fields
are the dense, inverted
facets
of a glaucous star.

I taste
and exhale them!

Wind's skin!
Where space,
into its chrysalis, contracts.

Amongst
its breathing minerals
I recognize
my mirror.

Lip.
Lips,
and the blind spine's
bright
shiver!

EYE

A cold drift through   the imageless.
A hand. Its voices. Making its hollow is echoless.

Each of us   are somewhere we   aren't;
are drilled   sequences
of changeless cloud. Replicated space.

Are the eye we move through that's never seen us.

BREATH VEGETAL

All verbs, verbs   of unravelling.
All light
   a darkening into ripeness; a   ripening
onto the tall   transparent stem.

                      Slipped crystals,
and the warm, wind-pitted sun. And the   lips

   suddenly limp
as the long hair spreads,
             in wet   bracelets, over   the arms.

PROSE 1

Arose.
Against the wind in glassy wheels and the shivering of the syca-
mores. Stretched in their rich spindles.
To enter. Forever press. The breath forced. The skin new.
The new vowels, mumbling with roots.
With branches.
With birds gliding into their own shadows.

That enter, clamoring.

That, wider. Into the white landscapes that forever lessen.

HELIX

Dawn
diamonds the wind!

O alive!
Alive,
and risking ourselves
on reaching
the Inevitable!

Thighs, boulders, lightning,
we're deep pods
of breath
breathing ourselves
into light!

My teeth! Your shoulders!

O flesh
in the throe of its flower,
the air's
spiralling meadow's,
our radiance
is what the wind-crystals sing,
and the black earth
echoes!

NOTES FROM AN ORCHARD

Had entered the orchard
         the full ice, the blue   celestite
                           of the flowering orchard.

                    •

Are the words wide, violent enough /   to realize
         our own innocence?

                    •

                    Risked myself

in the deafening splendor: the blood
         the harped blood of these inviolate
                              branches, that scar
         quilled, through silence.

                    •

A bee
      carves their cold, nubulous mass; adding

its octave. No poles,   dialectics in enormity;   only
these raw, threading vibrations: aimed
                     adamant   into themselves

                    •

Something,
            within me, was being waged. The vestige bones
                            of a lost voice!

The last
      and first wrestlers!

•

We're not inhuman enough to hear   what we hear (to
          touch   what, craving, we feel).

•

O bliss, its hideous tangle!   ammoniate   float!

          Inferno
          was what we'd made of it,
and shredded the   echo   of these worded-limbs
          the bough, euphoric, that   we couldn't ravish.

•

Be
swift. In the wind the flowers phosphorescing thicken.

          Something in me / that isn't mine
          would touch the chord

and shatter the rings   that rib me   in this   ear
                              of   darkness.

ISN'T / that's almost

     ISN'T
that's almost (its vastness, infinitesimal: a GLINT
  in the voice's wonderous shadows). ISN'T

that dreams itself: the translucent herd   of its
  kisses driven, ineluctable, the

EARTH GERMINAL o driven / into the absence that IS!

NOTES ON CONTRIBUTORS

A long interview with WALTER ABISH appeared in the December 1975 issue of *Fiction International,* and his "Self-Portrait" is included in *Individualists: Post Movement Art,* an anthology published this year by E. P. Dutton. New Directions has brought out his novel *Alphabetical Africa* (1974) and the short story collection *Minds Meet* (1975).

Biographical information on FRANCISCO BRINES will be found in the note preceding his "Ten Poems." LOUIS M. BOURNE's translations from the Spanish have appeared frequently in these pages. Resident in Madrid for the past several years, he is currently putting together an anthology of post-Civil War poetry.

COLEMAN DOWELL's *Island People,* excerpts of which have appeared in this anthology series, has just been published by New Directions. The Spanish-language edition of his *Mrs. October Was Here* (1973) is now being prepared by Ediciones Felmar (Madrid). Meanwhile, Dowell is completing work on his fourth novel, *Too Much Flesh and Jabez.*

Visual Beatitudes, LAWRENCE FERLINGHETTI's newest collection of poems, will be added to the New Directions list this fall. Owner and publisher of City Lights Books, he has for twenty years been a guiding light of the San Francisco cultural scene. And in fact, that city celebrated its first "Lawrence Ferlinghetti Day" early last summer.

180

A leading figure in contemporary Italian letters, FRANCO FORTINI was born in Florence in 1917 and, since 1945, has lived in Milan. His published work includes four books of poetry, two of narrative fiction, as well as several essay collections. He has, in addition, rendered into Italian the writings of Brecht, Eluard, Gide, Goethe, Proust, and Queneau, among others. MICHAEL HAMBURGER, who translated Fortini's "Five Poems," is the well-known British critic, poet, and anthologist.

JAMES B. HALL teaches at the University of California, Santa Cruz. *The Heart Within: Poems by James B. Hall,* his most recent book, was published in 1973 by Louisiana State University Press.

"Parcel of Wrists," says STEVE KATZ "is one piece from a concatenation of works I call *Moving Parts* that is near completion. I'm also working on a novel entitled *Keeper,* about a merchant seaman and his room of tiny bats." Katz's published novels include *The Exaggerations of Peter Prince* (Holt, 1968), *Creamy and Delicious* (Random House, 1970), and *Saw* (Knopf, 1972).

MICHAEL MCCLURE has been called "one of the most original and vital poets in America" by the British critic Eric Mottram. His most recent collections are *Jaguar Skies* (1975) and *September Blackberries* (1974), both published by New Directions. In addition to his verse and his novel *The Adept* (1971), McClure is also a prolific playwright. *General Gorgeous,* his newest work, was produced last November at the A. C. T. Theatre in San Francisco.

In his introduction to the combined volume of JAMES PURDY's *Color of Darkness* (Doubleday, 1974), the British critic Tony Tanner writes: "He is as much of a poet of bewildered youth as he is an elegiast of emotionally depleted age . . . And he takes us to a place where, at one time or another, we all have to go." Purdy has published eight full-length novels thus far, most recently *In a Shallow Grave* (Arbor House, 1975). His work was the subject of a special symposium held at last year's Modern Language Association gathering in San Francisco. *Children Is All,* a collection of two plays and ten short stories, is available as a New Directions Paperbook.

The Estonian poet ALEKSIS RANNIT was born in Kallaste in 1914. Resident in the United States since 1953, for the past fifteen years he has been Curator of Russian and East European Studies at the Library of Yale University. "Dry Radiance," his selected poems, was included in *ND25*, translated and introduced by HENRY LYMAN.

Biographical information about DELMORE SCHWARTZ can be found in the note preceding his verse play *Shenandoah*. His *Selected Poems: Summer Knowledge* and *The World Is a Wedding* (two short novels and five stories) are published by New Directions. Last year, the University of Chicago Press issued a paperbook edition of the *Selected Essays of Delmore Schwartz*.

GUSTAF SOBIN was born in Boston in 1935 and was graduated from Brown University in 1958. He has been living in France for the past thirteen years, writing poetry, film scenarios, and children's books (one of which, *The Tale of the Yellow Triangle,* was published by George Braziller in 1973), and translating from the French and Provençal. His "Seven Poems" mark the first significant appearance of his poetry in the United States.

GILBERT SORRENTINO was a recipient of a Creative Artists Public Service Grant for 1974-75 and the winner of a 1975 Fels Award, sponsored by the Coordinating Council of Literary Magazines. An excerpt from *Synthetic Ink,* his novel-in-progress, appeared in *ND30*. In 1973, New Directions brought out his book-length prose poem *Splendide-Hôtel* as a paperbook as well as in a signed, limited edition.

Information about each of the "Ten English Poets" can be found in the bibliographical section following their work. The selection was made by ANDREW CROZIER, whose own books include *Train Rides* (Ferry Press, 1968), *Walking on Grass* (Ferry Press, 1969), *The Veil Poem* (Burning Deck Books, 1973), and the anthology *In One Side & Out the Other* (Ferry Press, 1970).

New Directions Paperbooks

Complete descriptive catalog available free on request from
New Directions, 333 Sixth Avenue, New York 10014.   † Bilingual